AI Rookies Labs: Beginning NLP with Orange

Visual, No-Code Text Analysis

Data Analytics Curriculum, LLC

About the Publisher

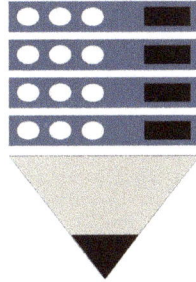

Data Analytics Curriculum

Data Analytics Curriculum, LLC creates approachable, visually engaging educational materials that make data science and technology accessible for learners from high school to college and independent study.

Please see our website or TPT online store for additional titles and resources such as slides, additional book forms, content (non lab) textbooks to accompany these labs, solution guides and other resources to help you teach and learn.

Additional resources available:

Website: https://www.dataanalyticscurriculum.com

Acknowledgement

This book makes use of Orange Data Mining software, developed by the Bioinformatics Laboratory at the University of Ljubljana. Orange is open-source software released under the GNU General Public License v3.

For more information, visit https://orange.biolab.si.

All screenshots, workflows, and examples based on Orange are used in compliance with this license.

Contents

Lab 1

Get Started with Orange

Orange is a free, open-source data mining tool that uses visual programming with Python in the background. It allows you to explore data analysis workflows without writing code. It is available for download at orangedatamining.com.

Because Orange runs on Python you must first have Python installed although Orange guides you through this if it does not detect a prior installation. Orange requires no coding unless advanced usage is intended although it does fully integrate with Python and understand the language.

Note Orange does a base installation. There are additional packages available that need to be installed as add ins for specific tasks (such as Text Analytics or Association Analysis).

1.1 Lesson Steps

Step 1: Starting Orange

When you first launch Orange a Welcome Screen appears.

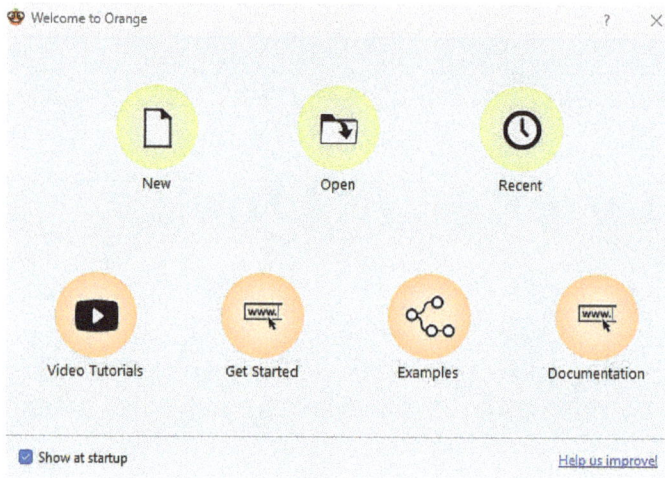

From here you have the options of starting a new workflow, opening a recent (workflow) file, or exploring documentation and tutorials Orange provides online. Select the option to start a new workflow.

Step 2: Orange Interface Overview

Let's get familiar with the Orange environment. There are two main components. On the right is the Canvas area (which is simply a blank white workspace which on start-up has nothing in it). On the left is a widget directory (the left panel). This is where you can obtain the widgets you need and drag and drop them onto the workspace. Note that the widgets are grouped by tasks (Data, Visualize, etc.).

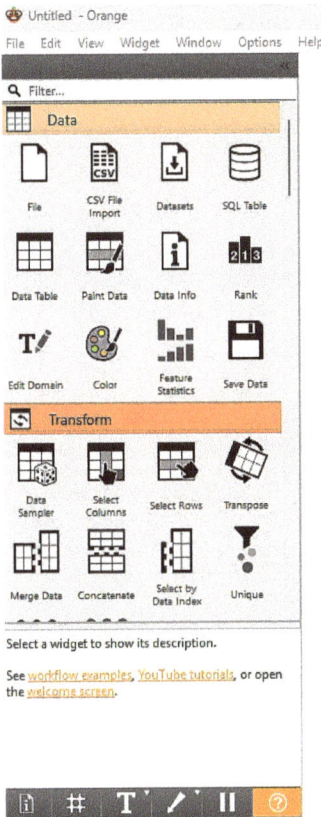

Step 3: Widgets

Widgets are modular tools for tasks like data import, analysis, and visualization. Underneath (and invisible to you) each widget is Python specific programming. When you use widgets you are effectively sending input and receiving output form the underlying Python code, but you do not need to do any coding to use Orange.

As you hover over the widgets it gives details on what each widget does (on the bottom left). Read the descriptions shown. Each widget has a specific role. For example, the File widget loads data from your computer, while Datasets can load example files. Understanding each widget's function helps you choose the right one for your task.

Step 4: Load Sample Data

Now let's create a practice workflow and get you ready to use Orange. Drag a Datasets widget from the Data group onto the Canvas.

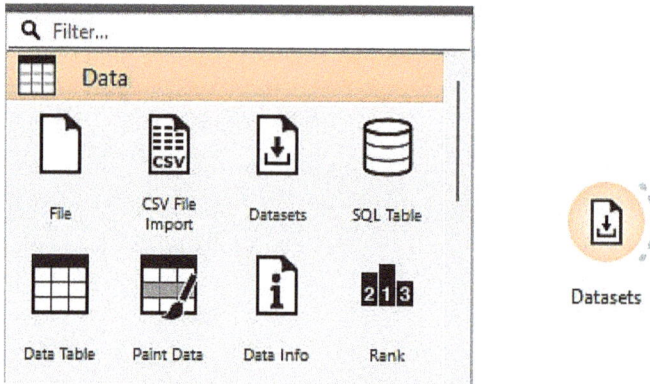

Double-click to open it and select Iris dataset which is built into the system (we are not yet loading external data).

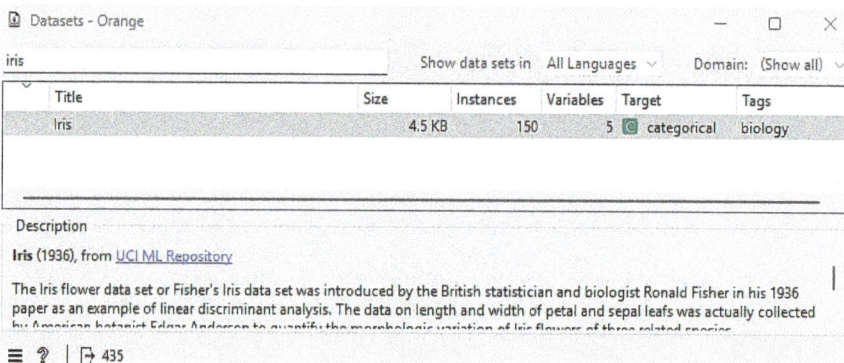

Step 5: View the Data

Add a Data Table widget to the canvas. Connect this to the Datasets widget.

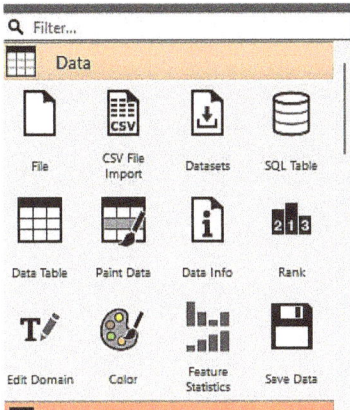

Click on the Data Table widget to view the data.

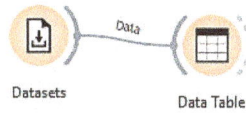

Step 6: Visualize the Data

From the Visualize group, drag a Scatter Plot widget onto the canvas. Connect the Data Table to the Scatter Plot.

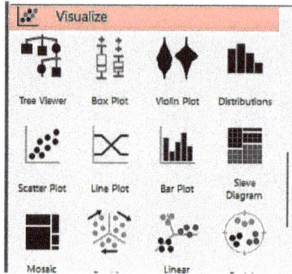

Double-click Scatter Plot to view the graph (play around with the graph axis and settings to explore more).

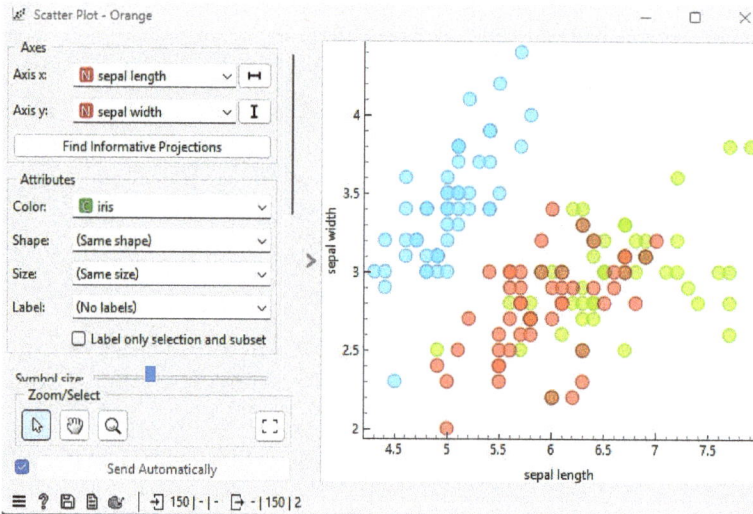

Step 7: Save Your Work

Go to File > Save As. Save the project with a name. Orange saves files as .ows (Orange Workflow Schema). You can also export results or create a journal for sharing.

Very importantly - once a workflow is setup and saved it can be used for different data simply by using a different dataset in the starting widget. This can be very helpful to not always have to start each workflow from scratch.

1.2 Wrap-Up

This lab was introduction to Orange's visual programming environment. It covered how to launch the app, add and connect widgets, load sample data, and view simple visualizations. Orange makes it simple to do analytics and you can build and reuse workflows, and you don't have to write code. Now you are ready to learn NLP.

Lab 2

Preprocessing Text

You can't really start analyzing text until you've cleaned it up a bit or in formal terms preprocessed it. Raw text is often messy and inconsistent, which makes it hard for any kind of analysis to work properly. So before doing anything advanced—like figuring out what a message is about or grouping similar texts—you need to go through a few basic cleanup steps.

In this exercise, you'll use Orange to do three of the most common text preprocessing tasks: breaking the text into individual words (tokenization), turning everything into lowercase so it's consistent, and getting rid of common filler words like "the" or "and" that don't add much meaning.

If the Text Mining add-on isn't visible in the widget menu and this is the first time using it, then it needs to be installed from Orange. To do this, go to the top menu, select Options ◉ Add-ons, and install the Text Mining package.

2.1 Lesson Steps

Step 0: Prepare data

Create a CSV file called Lab2Sample.csv using a text editor or spreadsheet tool. Use the content depicted here.

ID	Text
1	I love Orange for data mining!
2	Tokenization splits text into words.
3	Simple datasets make learning easy.
4	Text preprocessing is an important step.
5	Let's explore text mining together.

Step 1: Launch Orange

Open Orange and choose New to start a fresh workflow. Add a File widget to the canvas.

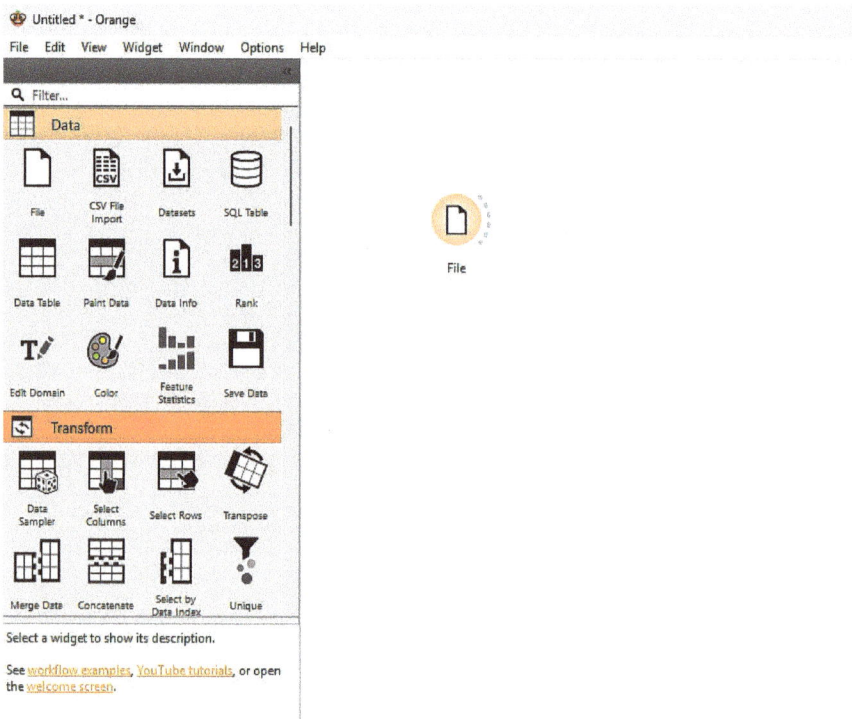

Step 2: Load Data

Open the widget and upload the Lab2Sample.csv file you just created. Orange should automatically detect the text column.

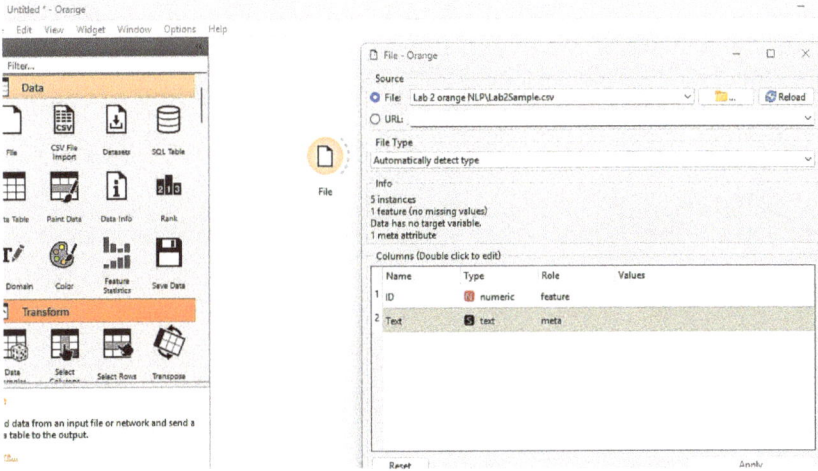

Step 3: Create Corpus

A Corpus is a data object that holds a collection of text documents and in order to use text documents for analysis you need to make a corpus. Add a Corpus widget to the canvas and connect it to the File widget. Next add a Corpus Viewer and connect it to the Corpus widget. Click on the Corpus Viewer to view the unprocessed text.

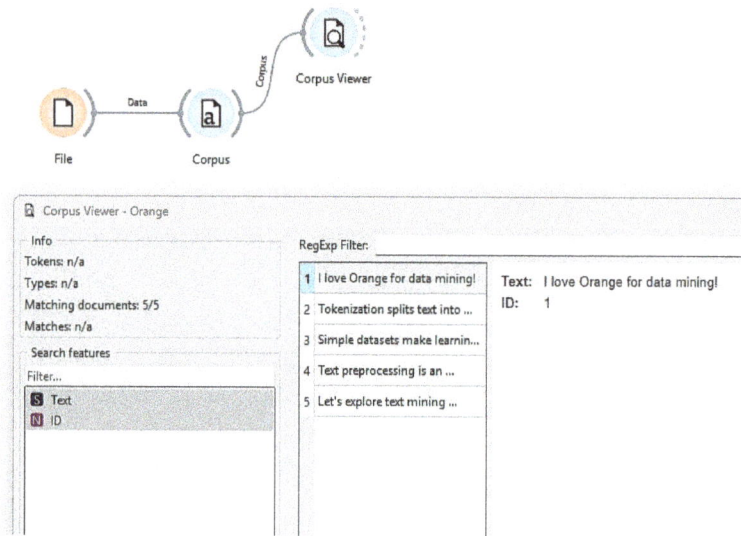

Step 4: Perform Word Tokenization

The first thing you'll do with the text is break it into smaller parts, usually individual words. This is called tokenization which turns blocks of text into pieces that can be analyzed. Without it, computers doing NLP analytics wouldn't know how to handle the content or recognize patterns.

To try this out, add a Preprocess Text widget to the canvas and connect it to the Corpus widget. When you open the Preprocess Text widget, you'll see a few default options already listed. Clear those out. Then add just the tokenization step.

Orange uses a regular expression method to do this by default. That means it follows a simple pattern to decide what counts as a word. The pattern it uses pulls out groups of letters, numbers, or underscores, and ignores things like punctuation and symbols.

Step 5: View the Tokenized Data

Connect the Preprocess Text widget to a new Corpus widget and connect this to a new Corpus Viewer Widget.

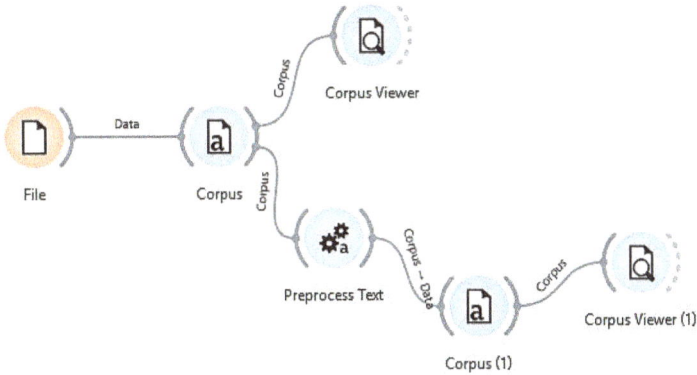

Open the Corpus Viewer to see the tokenized text. Note in order to see this
in the bottom left hand corner of the Corpus Viewer widget you must have
checked off the "Show Tokens & Tags" option.

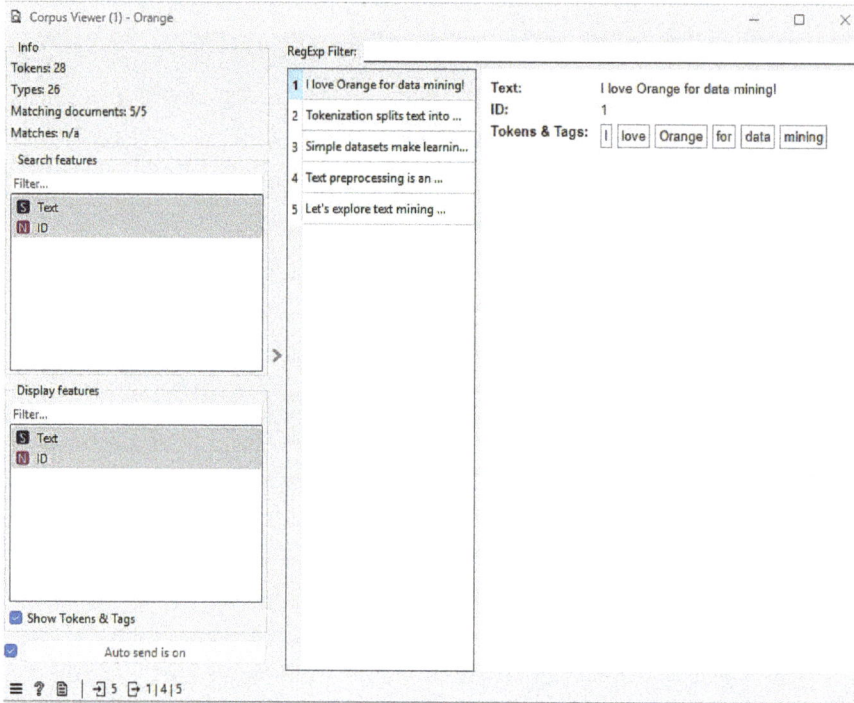

Now the text is tokenized (broken up into one word bits).

Step 6: Make Data Lowercase and View

The next thing to do is to make all text lowercase (so that Hi and hi are the same word). Add another Preprocess Text widget, connect it to a third (added) Corpus widget and connect that to a new Corpus Viewer.

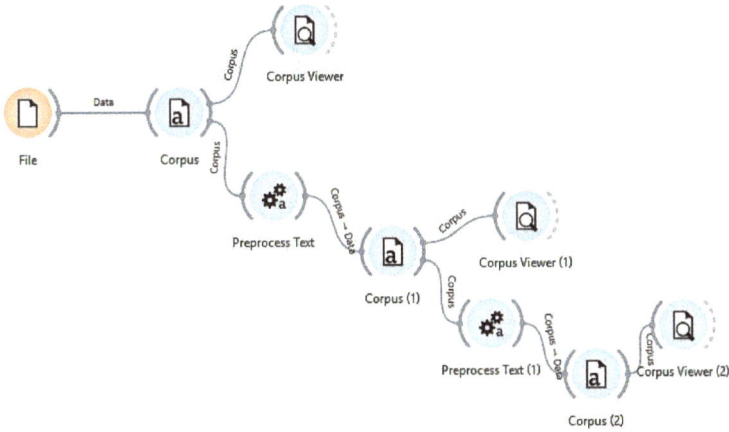

Set the Preprocess Text widget to have the Tokenization first step done prior and also add a Transformation step with lowercase checked off. Note the Preprocess Text widget performs operations in the order (top first) they are added on the right side (so Tokenization first, Transformation second). Sometimes this order matters in preparing text for analysis.

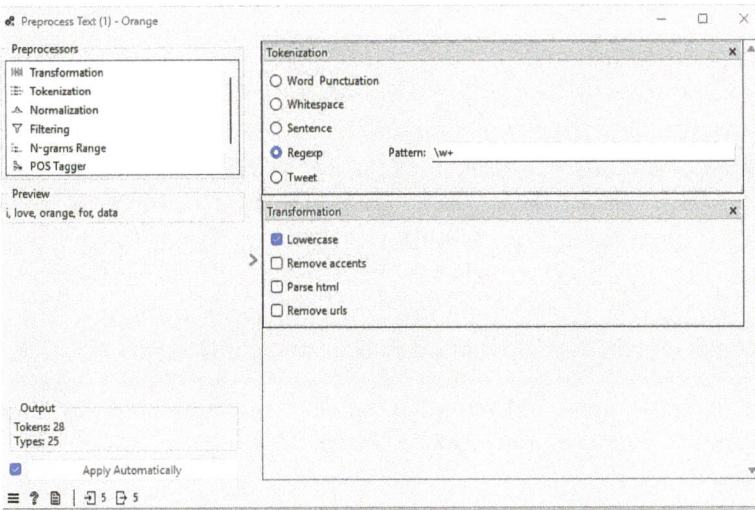

Open the Corpus viewer to see that all text is lowercase (compare to prior
views).

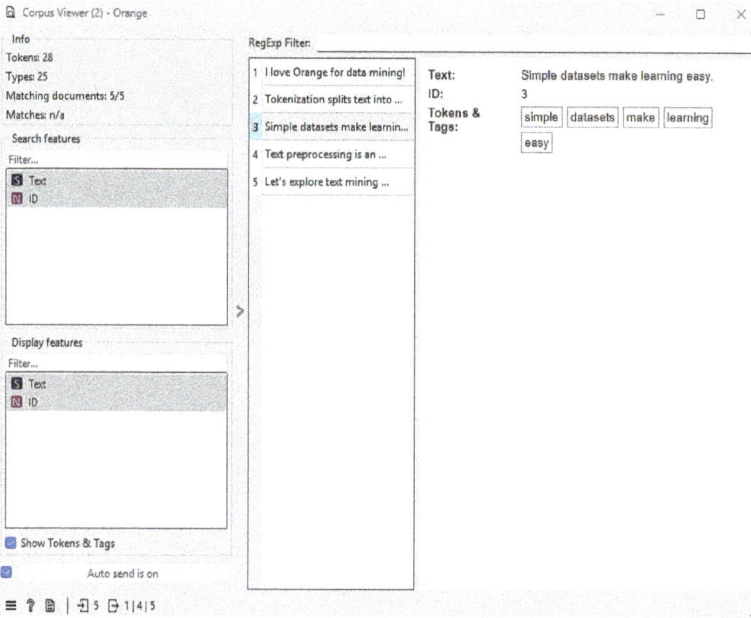

Step 7: Remove Stopwords

Our final step of basic preprocessing will be to remove stopwords. Stopwords
are the most common words in a language, like "the", "in", "is", or "and".
They are useful for grammar but usually don't add much meaning to the
analysis of a document. For example, if you are trying to find out what a
paragraph is really about, words like "the" or "and" are unlikely to help. In
text analysis, we often remove these stopwords to reduce noise and focus on
the important words that tell us more about the content.

Add another Preprocess Text widget, connect it to a new (added) Corpus widget and connect that to a new Corpus Viewer.

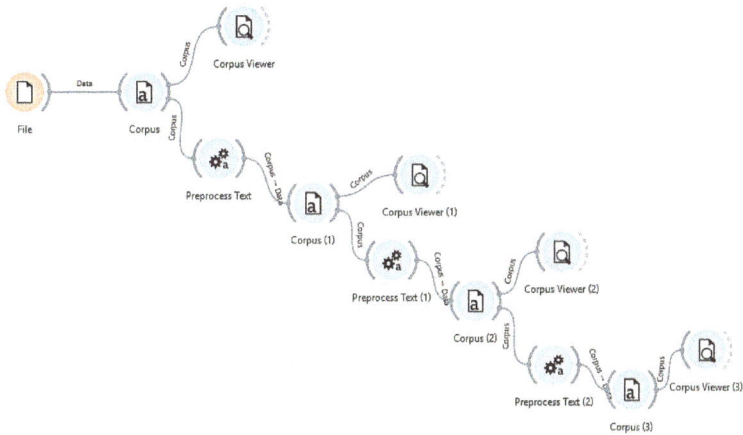

Open the new Preprocess Text widget and this time add an option Filtering and select stopwords. You'll also notice an upload field field on the right side of the widget. This allows you to upload your own list of stopwords, though in this example, we'll use the default list provided by Orange. A custom list would for example allow you to keep certain stop words if they had analytical meaning to you and you did not want them removed.

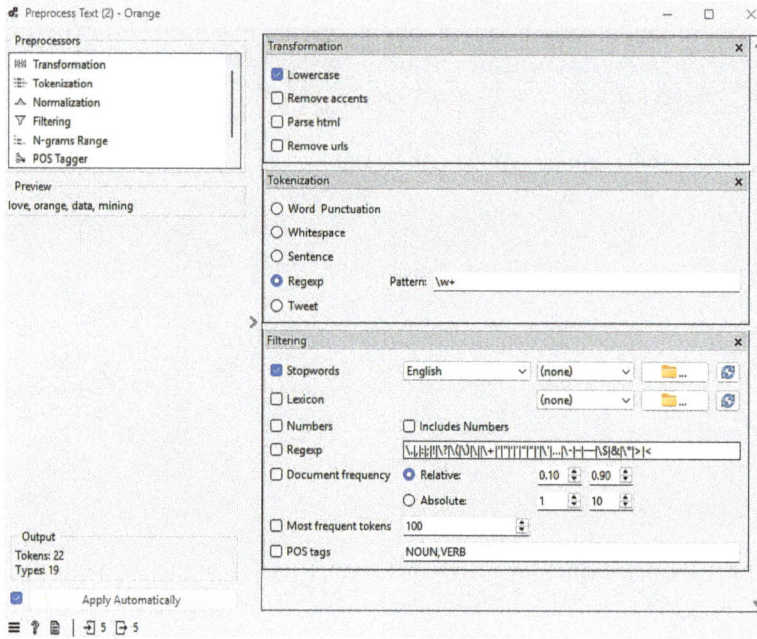

Step 8: View Final Preprocessed Data

Finally open the Corpus Viewer and see what the preprocessed text looks like
- it is all lower case, all tokenized and all stopwords have been removed. At
this stage it is ready for many analysis. Compare the final Corpus Viewer with
the first for the unprocessed text to confirm the difference.

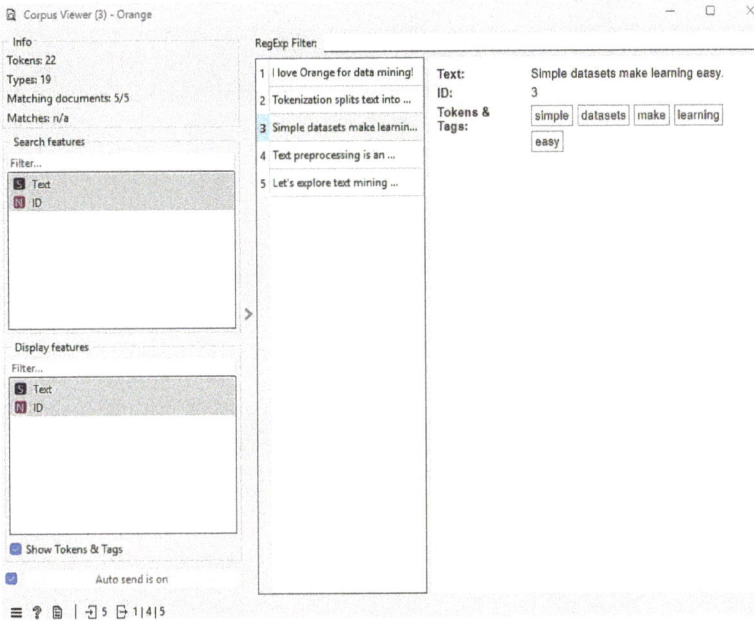

Note that we just did the preprocessing in multiple steps to train beginners. In reality in Orange often all steps would be done at once however this would not show exactly what the preprocessing does at each step.

2.2   Wrap-Up

This lab was a hands beginner introduction to how to take text data and prepare it so it can be used for analysis, known as preprocessing. For this we learned how to do three things: break up the text into component words, made everything lowercase, and omitted common words like "the" or "and" that don't add analytical value.

First, splitting the text into words—tokenization—helps the software treat each word as its own piece. Without that, it's all just a big chunk of text. Next we made everything lowercase, so "Data" and "data" don't get treated like different words, which would just mess things up later. And finally, we got rid of words that show up all the time but don't really help us figure out what the text is saying.

It was useful to see how the text changed step by step. Each part helps clean things up so later analytical tools —like the ones that group text or find patterns—can actually work the way they're supposed to.

2.3   Exercises

Let's practice the text preprocessing skills learned in this lesson.

Dataset 1: Social Media Posts
Uses dataset: social_posts.csv

1. Upload the dataset and view the original text using a Corpus Viewer. What are the first and last lines of text shown?

2. After applying tokenization, what does the tokenized version look like?

3. Add lowercasing to the preprocessing. What changes do you see in the tokens?

4. Apply stopword removal. What words remain?

5. Compare the output before and after preprocessing. What content was lost or transformed?

Dataset 2: Customer Service Reviews
Uses dataset: support_reviews.csv

6. What does the unprocessed text look like in the Corpus Viewer?

7. After tokenizing and lowercasing, how does it change?

8. Which words are removed by the stopword filter?

9. Does post 5 retain any adjectives after preprocessing? If so, list them.

10. Compare the total token count before and after preprocessing for post 3. What does this tell you?

Dataset 3: News Headlines
Uses dataset: news_headlines.csv

11. What words are tokenized from headline 1?

12. Which keywords remain in headline 2 after stopword removal?

13. Apply all three preprocessing steps. What is the final version of headline 3?

14. Compare headlines 4 and 5 after preprocessing. What types of words are retained?

15. How could preprocessing these headlines help improve the ability of a computer to search or categorize the topics in the headlines?

Lab 3

Stemming and Lemmatization

After you split the text into words, the next thing you usually do is some standardization to make those words simpler or more uniform. That's what normalization means. There are two popular ways to do this: stemming and lemmatization.

Stemming is kind of like chopping off the ends of words (kind of like what the rabbit did to the top of my garden plants last night....). Stemming just snips endings without worrying much about the actual meaning. So words like "running," "runs," and "runner" might all get cut down to "run" or sometimes even "runn." It's fast, but it's not always super accurate.

Lemmatization does more (and involves more processing). It looks at the word and how it's used to find the actual base form. For example, "running" becomes "run," but "better" actually becomes "good." Stemming can't do that.

Both of these help by shrinking down the number of different words you have to deal with. That way, it's easier for computers to spot patterns or group similar texts together. In this lab, you'll get to see both methods in action.

3.1   Lesson Steps

If the Text Mining add-on isn't visible in the left-side widget menu, you'll need to install it. To do this, go to the top menu, and find add-ins and install it from the Orange site (must be online).

Step 0: Prepare data

Create a data file with the words list below and name it normalize.csv.

word

running

runs

easily

fairly

children

better

connection

connections

Step 1: Setup

Open a new workflow in orange, add a File widget and upload normalize.csv.

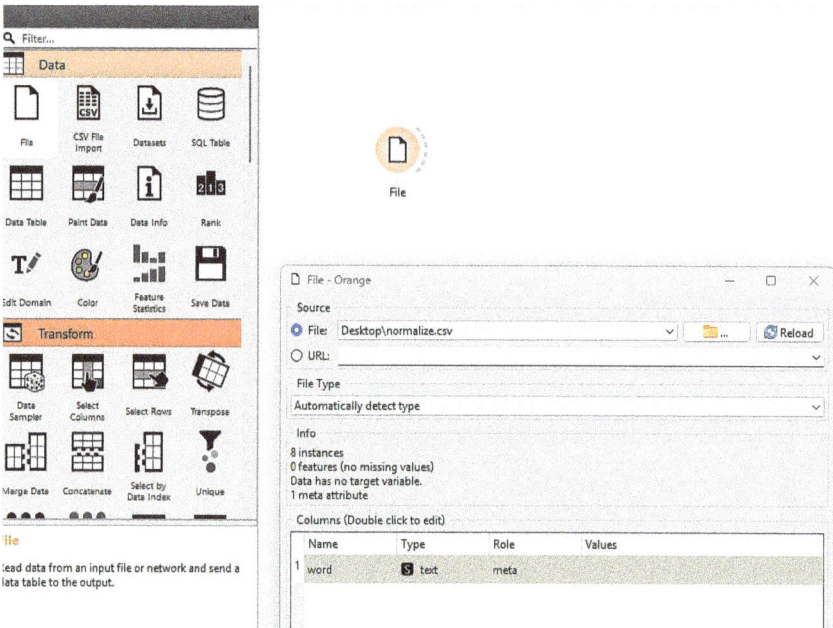

Step 2: Create Corpus

Add a Corpus widget and connect to the File widget. Add a Corpus View widget and connect to the corpus widget. Open the Corpus Viewer to check the data.

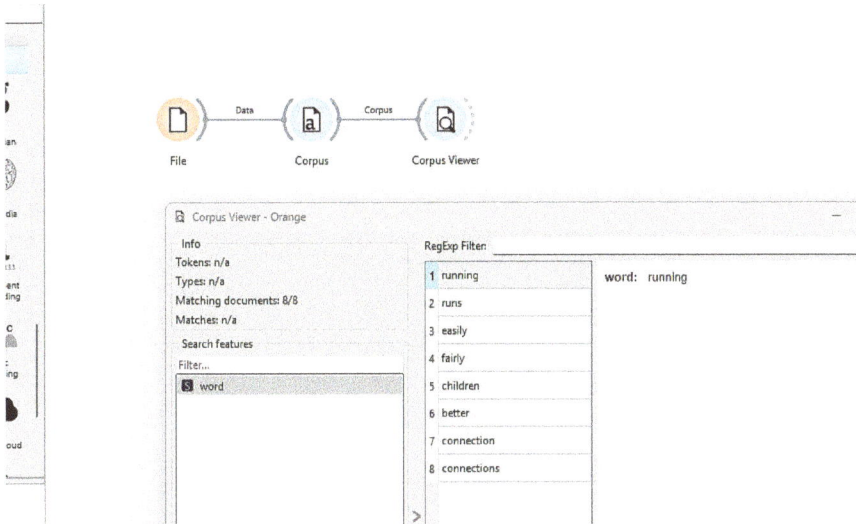

Step 3: Preprocess for Stemming

To perform stemming in Orange, add a new Preprocess Text widget and connect it to the Corpus. The Preprocess widget should (on the right side) have defaults for tokenization, lowercase and stopword filtering (if not add these, refer to lab 2-1). Add a Normalize section to the right side by clicking on it on the list option. It should appear last on the right side (you may need to scroll down). In the Normalize section that appears check Porter Stemmer.

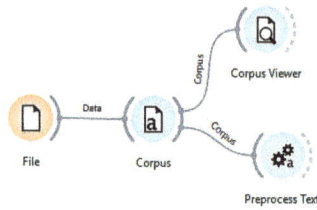

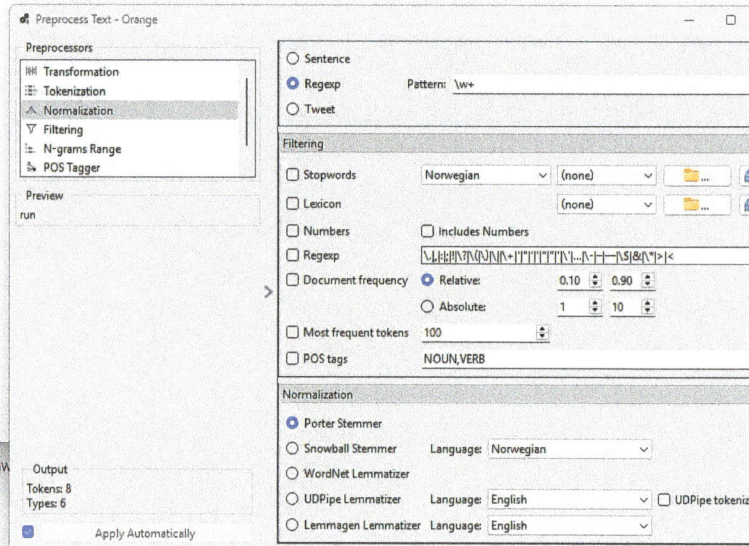

The Porter Stemmer is a popular stemming method. It applies a series of rule-based steps to strip suffixes from words—for example, it changes "caresses" to "caress," "ponies" to "poni," and "running" to "run"—by matching and replacing common endings like -ing, -ed, or -es in a fixed sequence.

Step 4: View Stemming Results

Add a Corpus Viewer widget and connect it to the output of the Preprocess Text widget. Open the Corpus Viewer to see the stemmed words. You will notice that some words look unusual, like "easily" becoming "easili". This is normal because stemming removes word endings using simple rules without understanding grammar. Notice for word 7 'connection' has been stemmed to 'connect' (make sure show tokens and tags is checked).

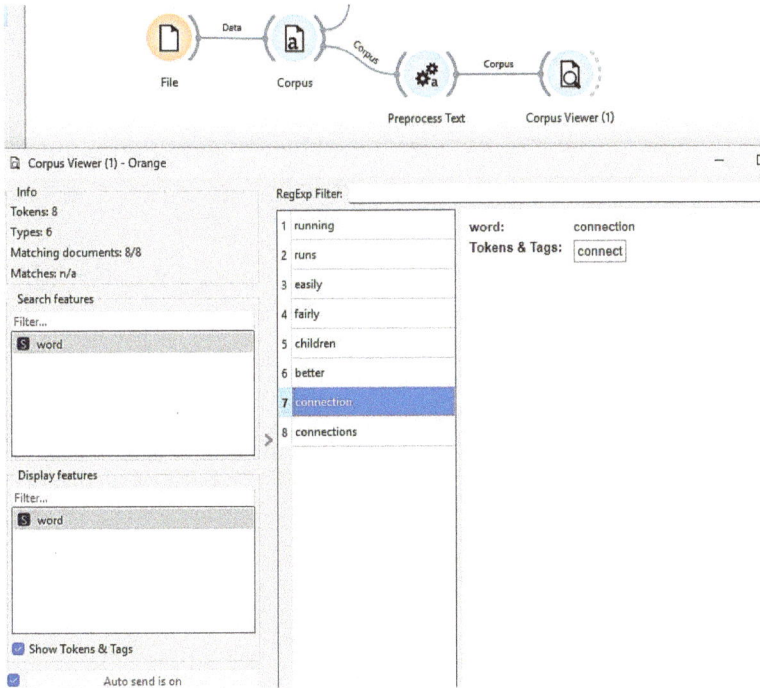

Step 5: Preprocess for Lemmatization

To perform lemmatization in Orange, add a new Preprocess Text widget and connect it to the Corpus. In this widget, add a Normalize section by clicking on it on the list option. In the Normalize section that appears check WordNet Lemmatizer.

The WordNet Lemmatizer reduces words to their base or dictionary form, known as a lemma. It uses the WordNet lexical database and considers the word's context and part of speech, so it returns valid words—for example, it turns "running" into "run" but leaves "ran" unchanged.

Step 6: View Lemmatization Results

Add a new Corpus Viewer widget and connect it to the output of the new Preprocess Text widget. Open the Corpus Viewer to see the lemmatized text. You'll notice that the words are now proper dictionary forms, such as "children" becoming "child" and "runs" becoming "run".

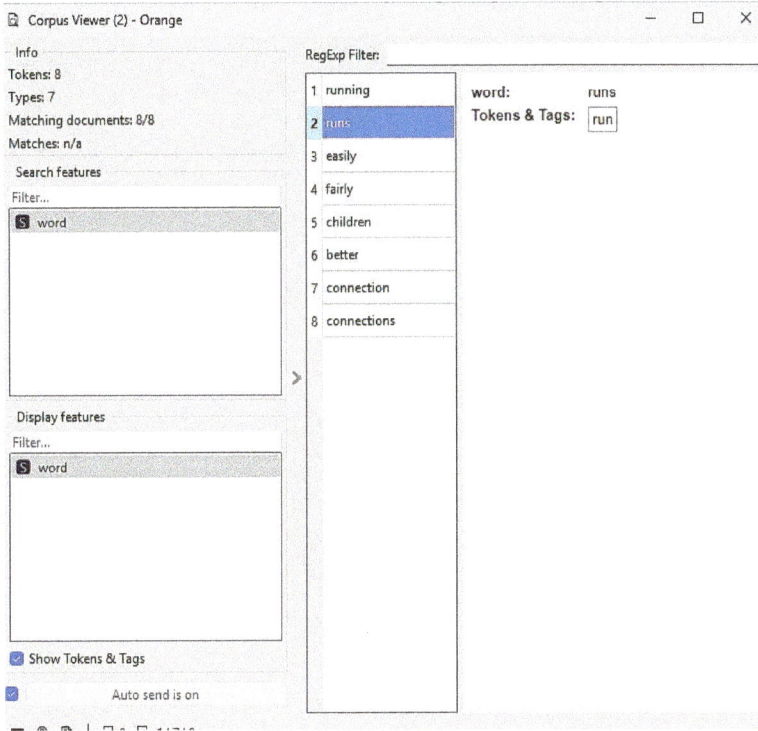

Step 7: Compare

Look at the Corpus Viewer widget outputs side by side to compare results for each word.

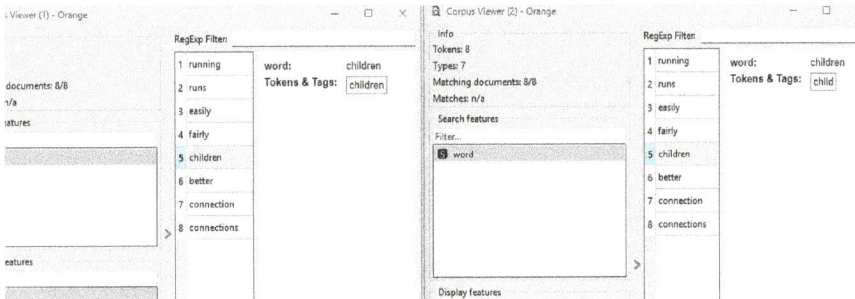

3.2 Wrap-Up

In this lab, you discovered two different ways to simplify words for analyzing text. One's called stemming — it's kind of a fast and rough approach where you basically just cut off the endings of words without really thinking about what they mean. The other one, lemmatization, is a bit more thoughtful; it actually looks at how the word is used in the sentence to figure out the proper base form.

You probably saw that these two do change words differently, and that's actually important depending on what you want to do. If speed is what matters and you don't need everything perfect, stemming's fine. But if you want to be more accurate and really get the right word forms to understand things better, lemmatization's the way to go.

3.3 Exercises

Stemming and Lemmatization

Let's practice normalizing text!

Dataset 1: Sports Terms

Create a CSV file named sports_words.csv with the following content:

```
word
playing
played
player
matches
winning
quickly
fairly
better
```

1. Import sports_words.csv into Orange and apply stemming. Paste a screenshot of the Corpus Viewer showing stemmed results.
2. What is the stemmed form of "playing"? Explain why it looks the way it does.
3. Now apply lemmatization on the same dataset. Paste a screenshot of the Corpus Viewer showing lemmatized results.
4. How do the outputs for "better" and "fairly" differ between stemming and lemmatization?
5. Which method—stemming or lemmatization—produced more readable or meaningful results in this case? Explain briefly.

Dataset 2: Technology Words

Create a CSV file named tech_words.csv with the following content:

```
word
computing
computes
computer
connected
connections
digitally
```

```
processing
faster
```

6. Apply stemming and show the Corpus Viewer output.
7. What happened to the words "connected" and "connections" after stemming?
8. Apply lemmatization to the same dataset and show the results.
9. What is the lemmatized form of "digitally"? How is it different from the stemmed version?
10. Based on this dataset, which normalization method might be more appropriate for understanding document topics? Why?

Dataset 3: Emotions and Behavior

Create a CSV file named emotion_words.csv with the following content:

```
word
happier
crying
laughed
kindness
loving
anger
feeling
cares
```

11. Apply both stemming and lemmatization. For each, note how the words "happier," "crying," and "kindness" were transformed. Show outputs and explain.
12. Which transformation (stemming or lemmatization) preserved emotional meaning more accurately in this set? Support your answer with examples.

Lab 4

Encoding Text

Encoding is just a fancy way of saying you're turning words into numbers so computers can actually do something with them. When we deal with language on computers, we need to change text into a form that machines can get — that's what encoding does.

Two of the most common ways to encode words are called bag of words and TF-IDF. Bag of words is kind of simple — it just counts how many times each word pops up in whatever you're looking at. It doesn't care about the order or grammar, just counts. It's easy to use and works okay for lots of things, but it doesn't know which words are actually important.

TF-IDF tries to fix that by saying, "Hey, words that show up everywhere aren't that helpful," and it lowers their score. Words that don't show up as much get a higher score, so it highlights the stuff that really stands out.

In this lab, you'll use Orange to check out both ways, see how they turn your text into numbers, and get things ready for whatever you want to do next, like grouping or sorting the data.

4.1 Lesson Steps

Step 1: Create a New Workflow

Start Orange and click on New to begin a new workflow. Add a Create Corpus widget to the canvas (under the Text Mining menu).

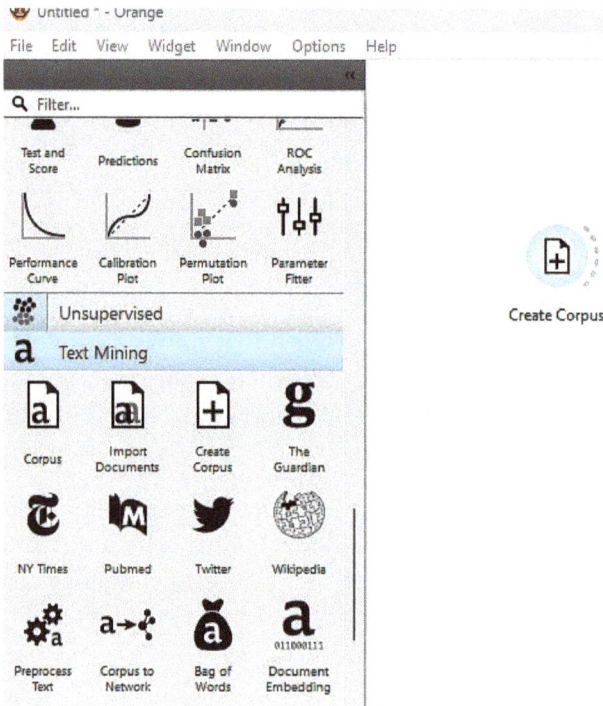

Step 2: Input the Text Data

You can manually input simple documents directly using the Create Corpus widget. Open the Create Corpus widget and manually add:

Document 1: I like apples

Document 2: I like oranges

Document 3: I like bananas

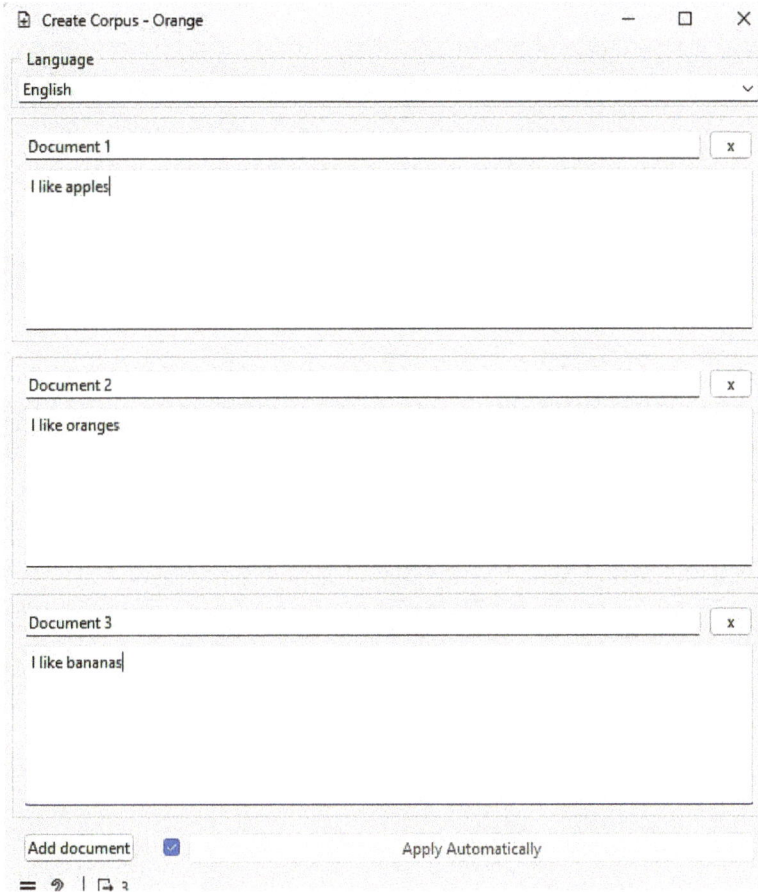

Step 3: Preprocess the Text

Add a Preprocess Text widget and connect it to the Create Corpus widget.

Open Preprocess Text and set as depicted. It should make text lowercase, tokenize the data and remove stopwords (covered in lab 2-1)

Step 4: Apply Bag of Words Encoder

Add a Bag of Words widget and connect it to the Preprocess Text widget and open the Bag of Words widget to view the default settings.

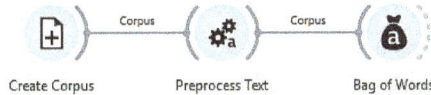

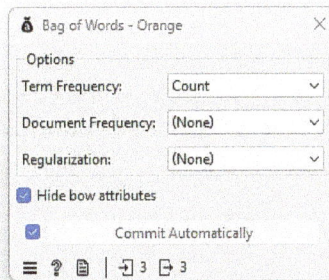

The Bag of Words widget converts text data into a numerical format by creating a document-term matrix, which can then be used in machine learning models. By default, it will preprocess text. It also strips out punctuation and ignores word order, meaning it treats the text as just a "bag" of words without context. Each document is then represented as a row in a matrix, with columns corresponding to unique words. The numeric encoded values indicating how many times each word appears in the document.

Step 5: View the Bag of Words

Add a Data Table to the workflow connected to the bag of words and open it.

bow-feature hidden include skip-normalization title	Title True	Document True	{...}
1	Document 1	I like apples	apples, like
2	Document 2	I like oranges	like, oranges
3	Document 3	I like bananas	bananas, like

This table displays the processed output from the Bag of Words (BoW). Each row corresponds to a document. The rightmost {...} column represents a sparse vector, which encodes the presence of words numerically, forming a document-term matrix.

Step 6: Word Cloud of BOW

For an addition view, also add a Word Cloud widget to the Bag of Words and click on it to view the Word Cloud.

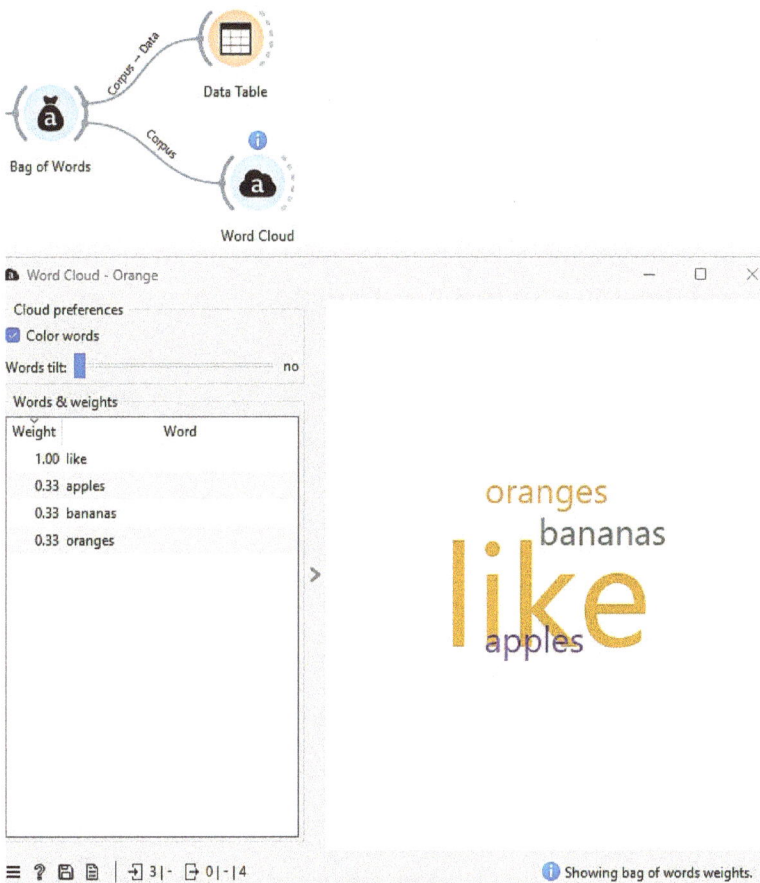

A Word Cloud visually represents the most frequent words from a set of doc-uments processed. The BoW approach converts text into a Document-Term Matrix (DTM), which counts word occurrences across all documents. The Word Cloud then uses this matrix to display words, where larger words ap-pear more frequently or have higher weight (such as TF-IDF scores). This makes it easy to spot dominant terms in the dataset at a glance. Essentially, it's a quick visual summary of word importance.

Step 7: Setup TF IDF Encoder

Add a second Bag of Words widget to the workflow from step also connected to the preprocess widget. Open this and set the document frequency to IDF (Term Frequency Inverse Document Frequency) which will instead compute the DTM using the TF IDF method (not bag of words) as Orange will apply the TF-IDF transformation instead of plain term counts.

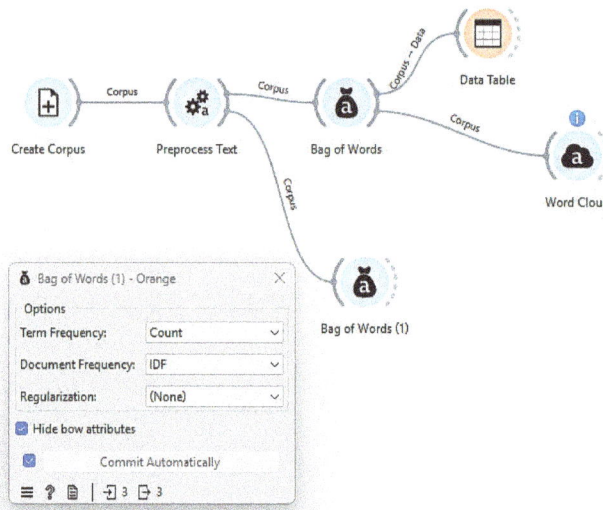

Bag of Words is basically just counting how many times each word shows up in your text. The thing is, it treats all words the same—even super common ones like "the" or "and." That can be a problem because those words show up everywhere and might hide the more important words that actually tell you what the text is about.

TF-IDF tries to fix that by giving less weight to words that appear a lot in lots of documents, and more weight to words that are rare or unique. This way, it helps bring out the words that really matter for understanding or sorting the text.

Because of this, TF-IDF usually does better when you want to search through text, group similar documents, or figure out the topics. So in short, Bag of Words shows you what's common, and TF-IDF helps you find the stuff that actually counts.

Step 8: View the TF IDF Results

Add a Data Table and connect it to the second bag of words. Open it to view results.

The numbers shown in the right column represent TF-IDF (Term Frequency–Inverse Document Frequency) scores for individual words in each document. These scores reflect how important a word is within a specific document compared to its importance across the entire collection of documents.

A higher score means the word appears frequently in one document but rarely in others, making it more informative. For example, in Document 1 ("I like apples"), the word "apples" has a TF-IDF score of approximately 1.09861. This is calculated by first determining the term frequency (TF), which is 1 because "apples" appears once in the document. Then, the inverse document frequency (IDF) is calculated using the formula $\log(N / df)$, where N is the total number of documents (3 in this case) and df is the number of documents containing the word "apples" (which is 1). So, the IDF is $\log(3 / 1) = \log(3) \approx 1.09861$. The TF-IDF score is then TF × IDF = 1 × 1.09861 = 1.09861. This means "apples" is unique to Document 1 and therefore carries more weight in identifying or describing that document.

Step 9: Word Cloud of TFIDF

Also add a Word Cloud widget to the Bag of Words (set for the TFIDF) and click on it to view the Word Cloud.

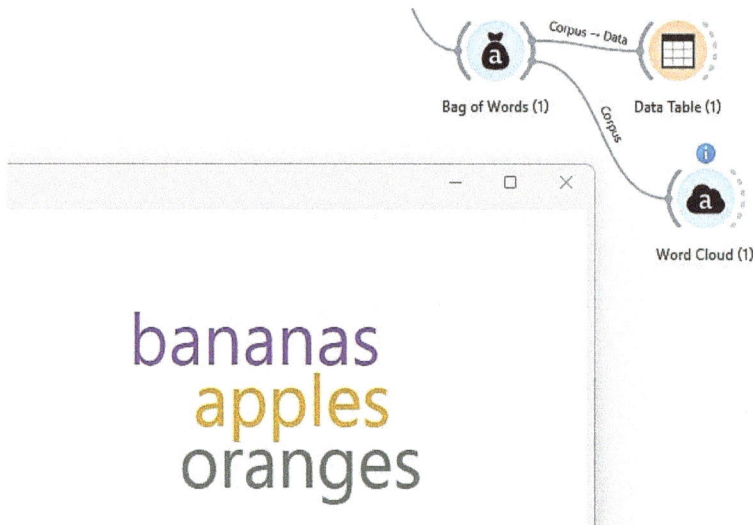

This word cloud shows what happens when you use TF-IDF to analyze text in Orange. The words "apples," "bananas," and "oranges" show up here because TF-IDF marks them as the most meaningful. Each of these words has a weight of 0.37, which basically means they stand out after the data's been normalized. TF-IDF picks out unique words as more important. Meanwhile, common words like "like" that appear in every document get low or zero scores and don't make it into the word cloud.

TF-IDF is good to find the words that really set one document apart from others. It filters out common filler words. On the other hand, Bag of Words is simpler and can work well if you just want a quick look at word frequency.

4.2 Wrap-Up

In this lab, you worked with two key ways to turn text into something machines can understand: bag of words (BoW) and TF-IDF. While using Orange, you saw that BoW simply counts how often each word appears in a document. TF-IDF gives more importance to words that are less common across the whole set of documents. Results of encodiing can be viewed using Data Table and Word Cloud tools, which helped you get a better feel for what the text is really saying.

These methods are important first steps for things like sorting texts into categories, grouping similar ones together, or finding common themes. Knowing the difference between BoW and TF-IDF will come in handy as you decide how best to pull out useful information from your text data.

4.3   Exercises

Encoding Text

Let's practice encoding techniques!

Dataset 1: Animal Facts

Use the Create Corpus widget in Orange to enter the following short documents:

- Document 1: *Elephants are the largest land animals on Earth.*
- Document 2: *Giraffes have long necks to reach high leaves.*
- Document 3: *Cheetahs are the fastest land animals.*

Once you've entered the text, connect it to a Preprocess Text widget. In the preprocessing settings, make sure to lowercase the text, tokenize the data, and remove stopwords. Then connect a Bag of Words widget to the output. To view the results, use both a Data Table and a Word Cloud connected to the BoW widget.

1. Paste the BoW Data Table output.
2. Which word appears in more than one document?
3. How many unique tokens are created in the BoW matrix?
4. What does the number "1" in the BoW output represent?
5. Paste the Word Cloud generated from BoW. What is the most frequent word?

Dataset 2: Travel Tips

Clear your previous workflow or create a new one, then enter this new set of documents in the Create Corpus widget:

- Document 1: *Pack light and bring only essentials.*
- Document 2: *Always carry your passport and identification.*
- Document 3: *Stay hydrated and rest during long trips.*

After entering the text, again connect a Preprocess Text widget with the same settings as before: lowercase, tokenize, and remove stopwords. Then add a TF-IDF widget to process the output of the preprocessor. Use a Data Table and Word Cloud to explore and display the results.

6. Paste the TF-IDF Data Table output.

7. What is the highest TF-IDF value and which word is it associated with?
8. Why does "your" likely have a lower TF-IDF value?
9. Paste the TF-IDF Word Cloud. How does it differ from the BoW one?
10. Name one advantage of TF-IDF over BoW based on your results.

Lab 5

Sentiment Analysis (Rule Based)

Sentiment analysis is a way for computers to estimate what kind of feeling or attitude a piece of text has. People use it all the time to check out stuff like reviews, tweets, or surveys to see what folks are really thinking or feeling. It can help businesses or researchers figure out if people like something or not and can be very important for things like market research.

There are two main ways to do sentiment analysis. The first is so-called rule-based. For rule based sentiment analysis a lexicon or rule book is used to map words to their sentiment. For example, the word "good," it thinks positive, but if there's a "not" before it, like "not good," it changes things around. This method is pretty easy to understand but can get confused by tricky language — like sarcasm or subtle jokes.

The second method is with machine learning. Here the computer looks at lots of examples where there is some indicator of the feeling, and learns patterns (hence, machine 'learning'). Machine learning methods usually perform better, but they take a lot more data and power to train, and it's not always easy to see why they make the decisions they do. Rule based methods are more simplistic and straightforward.

This lab will explore rule based sentiment analysis and the subsequent lab explores machine learning based sentiment analysis and how they can be implemented using Orange.

5.1 Lesson Steps

Step 1: Load the Dataset

To begin sentiment analysis in Orange, first add a Corpus widget. Use the Corpus widget to load the bakery_reviews.csv file. Make sure the Review column is set to Text.

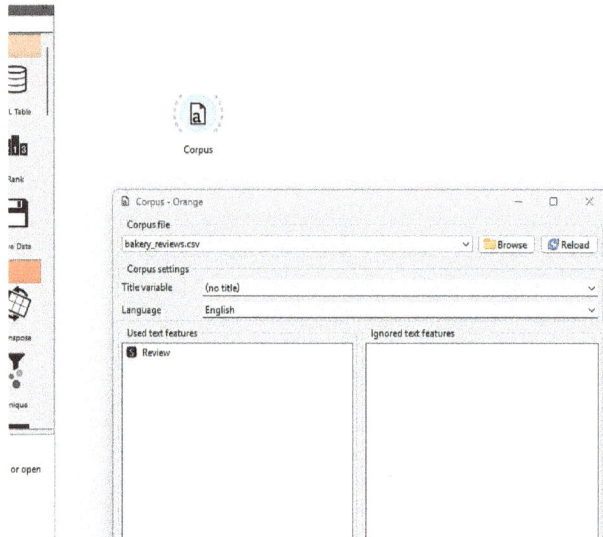

Step 2: Preprocess

Add the Preprocess Text widget. Connect it to the Corpus widget Use the default setting shown (adjust to this if this is not the default setting you see). This will make the text lower case, tokenize it and remove stop words.

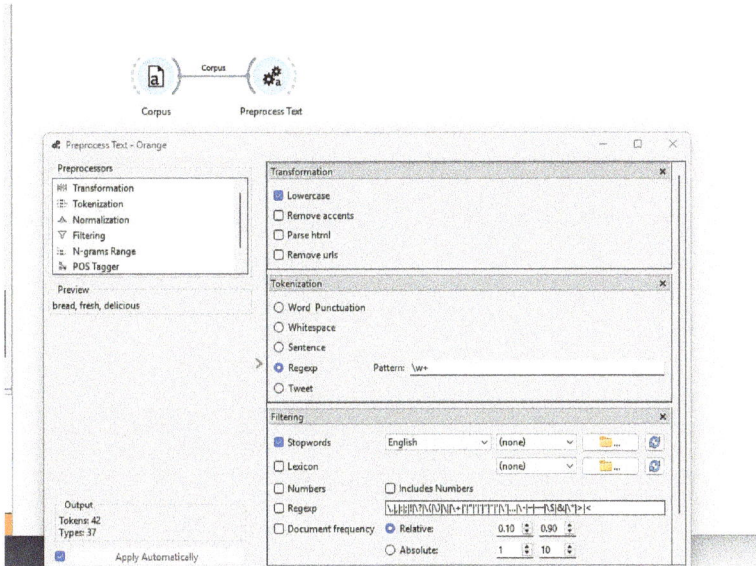

Step 3: Sentiment Analysis – VADER

Add a Sentiment Analysis widget (under Text Mining). Connect it to Preprocess Text widget. Open it up and the default method should be set to VADER (if not change it).

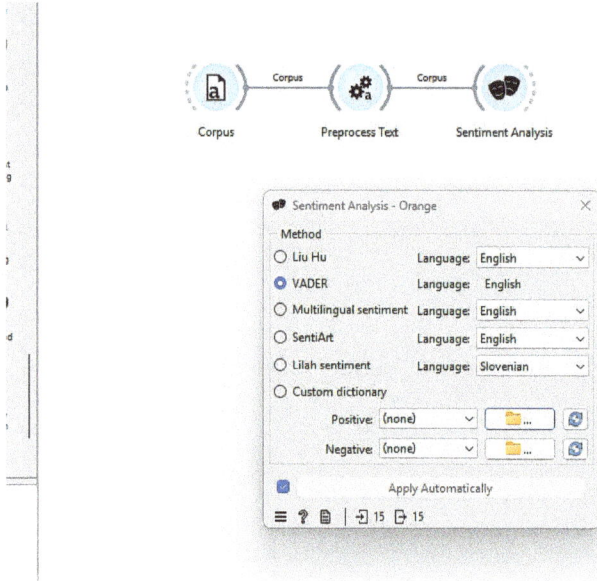

VADER (Valence Aware Dictionary and sEntiment Reasoner) is a tool used to find out if a piece of text is positive, negative, or neutral. It is especially good for short, casual messages like tweets, comments, or reviews. VADER uses a list of words that have been rated by people for how positive or negative they are. It also understands things like capital letters, punctuation (like "!!!"), and words that change meaning, such as "not" or "very." For example, it knows that "not bad" means something positive, not negative. VADER gives four results: one for how positive, negative, or neutral the text is, and a final number called the compound score that sums everything up between –1 (very negative) and +1 (very positive). It's a fast and easy way to check the feeling behind a sentence without needing to train a machine learning model.

Step 4: Results – VADER method

Add a Data Table and connect it to the Sentiment Analysis widget. Open to view results.

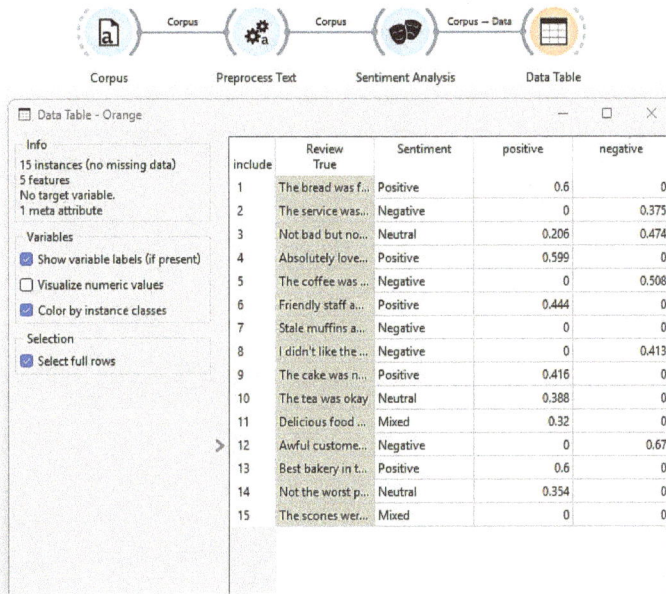

include	Review True	Sentiment	positive	negative
1	The bread was f...	Positive	0.6	0
2	The service was...	Negative	0	0.375
3	Not bad but no...	Neutral	0.206	0.474
4	Absolutely love...	Positive	0.599	0
5	The coffee was ...	Negative	0	0.508
6	Friendly staff a...	Positive	0.444	0
7	Stale muffins a...	Negative	0	0
8	I didn't like the ...	Negative	0	0.413
9	The cake was n...	Positive	0.416	0
10	The tea was okay	Neutral	0.388	0
11	Delicious food ...	Mixed	0.32	0
12	Awful custome...	Negative	0	0.67
13	Best bakery in t...	Positive	0.6	0
14	Not the worst p...	Neutral	0.354	0
15	The scones wer...	Mixed	0	0

Info: 15 instances (no missing data); 5 features; No target variable; 1 meta attribute.

Variables: Show variable labels (if present); Visualize numeric values; Color by instance classes.

Selection: Select full rows.

Results of VADER sentiment analysis are now displayed in Data Table. Each row represents a single review or sentence from the dataset. In the column labeled "Review", we see the text of the review.

The Sentiment column shows the overall predicted tone of each review—either Positive, Negative, Neutral, or Mixed. This label is based on how strongly the review leans toward positive or negative wording. The columns "positive" and "negative" display numerical scores given by VADER.

These scores reflect the strength of positive or negative sentiment found in the review. A score of 0.6 in the positive column means the review has a fairly strong positive tone, while 0.508 in the negative column shows strong negativity. If both positive and negative scores are present (e.g., row 11), the overall sentiment might be Mixed.

Step 5: View Results – VADER method

To get a feel for which words drive positive and negative sentiment you can

select only those rows and display them in a word cloud. To do this add a
Select Rows widget to the workflow and connect it the Sentiment Analysis
widget then add a Word Cloud widget and connect this as shown. Note for
the connector from the Select Rows to the Word Cloud it should be set to
connect Matching Data and Corpus (click on connector not widget to set this).

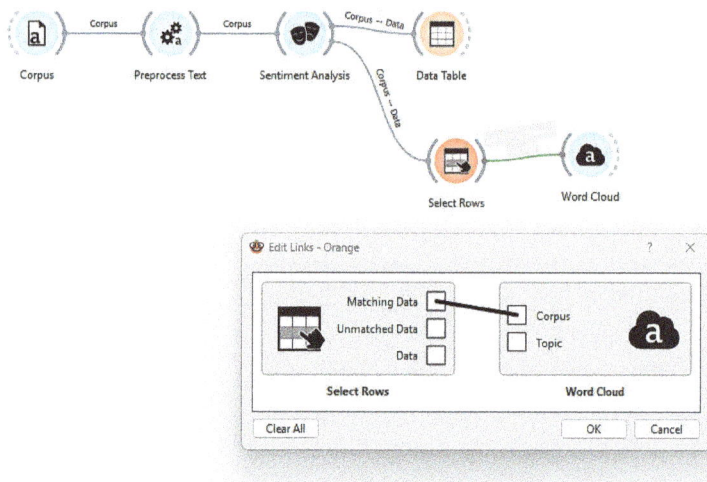

Now you can experiment with filtering for a sentiment and seeing what words
appear in the Word Cloud associated with that sentiment.

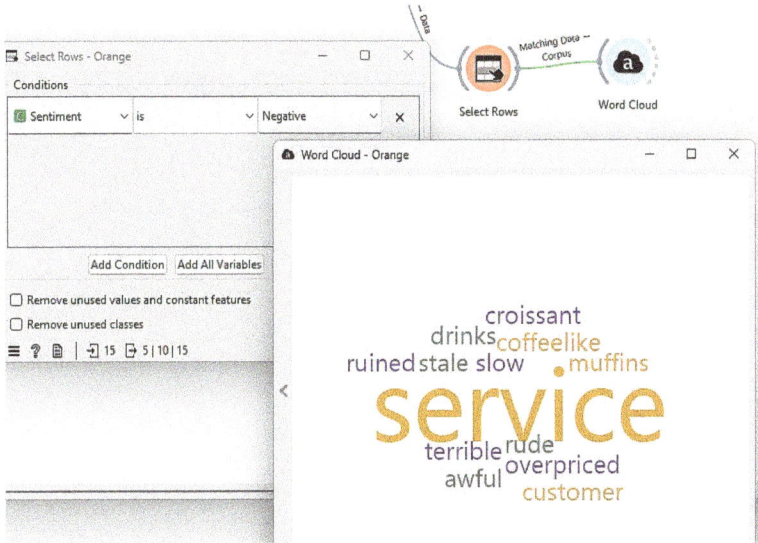

Step 6: Sentiment Analysis – LH

There are several methods for performing rule based sentiment analysis, and it's useful to explore different ones because no single method works best for every situation. Let's look at another method.

Add a second Sentiment Analysis widget to the workflow and connect it to the Preprocess Text widget. Click on this and change the setting to the Liu Hu (LH) method.

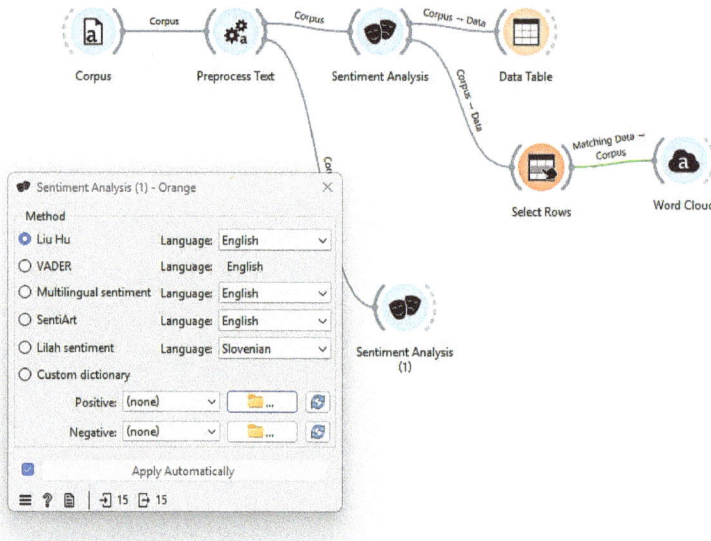

The Liu-Hu (LH) method and VADER are both tools used for finding out whether a piece of text is positive, negative, or neutral, but they work in different ways. LH just looks at how many good or bad words are in a piece of text, and then it decides if it's positive or negative based on which one shows up more. It's quick and kind of basic. But the problem is, it doesn't really understand meaning. Like if someone says "not good," it might still think that's a good thing just because "good" is on the happy list.

VADER still looks for positive and negative words, but it also checks for stuff like how strong the feeling is, and it pays attention to things like the word "not," all caps, exclamation points, and even emojis. That helps it do a better job with casual text — stuff like tweets or reviews where people don't always write formally. So, while LH is simple and fine for basic things, VADER's better if the language is more emotional or messy.

Step 7: Examine Results – LH method

Add a second Data Table widget and connect it to the Sentiment Analysis widget. Open this to examine the results.

		Review True	Sentiment	sentiment
include				
	1	The bread was f...	Positive	66.6667
	2	The service was...	Negative	-66.6667
	3	Not bad but no...	Neutral	0
	4	Absolutely love...	Positive	33.3333
	5	The coffee was ...	Negative	-50
	6	Friendly staff a...	Positive	50
	7	Stale muffins a...	Negative	-50
	8	I didn't like the ...	Negative	50
	9	The cake was n...	Positive	-50
	10	The tea was okay	Neutral	0
	11	Delicious food ...	Mixed	0
	12	Awful custome...	Negative	-50
	13	Best bakery in t...	Positive	33.3333
	14	Not the worst p...	Neutral	-50
	15	The scones wer...	Mixed	0

Info
15 instances (no missing data)
2 features
No target variable.
1 meta attribute

Variables
☑ Show variable labels (if present)
☐ Visualize numeric values
☑ Color by instance classes

Selection
☑ Select full rows

With the LH method, what it basically does is go through each review, finds the words that have a positive or negative meaning, adds up their values, and then evens it out to get one overall score. If the result is above zero, that means the review's mostly positive. If it's below zero, it's mostly negative. And if it's right around zero, it's neutral.

For example, something like "The bread was fantastic!" might get a pretty high score — like 66.67 — which shows it's really positive. But something like "The service was awful" might end up at -66.67, which is clearly negative. If a review has both kinds of words, like "Delicious food, but terrible service," it could get labeled as Mixed.

These scores make it easier to see how people feel overall, so you can do things like filter out only the good reviews to make a word cloud, or average the scores across different products or time ranges to spot trends.

Step 8: Visualize Results – LH method

Add a Heat Map widget (visualization menu) and connect it to the Data Table with the LH results.

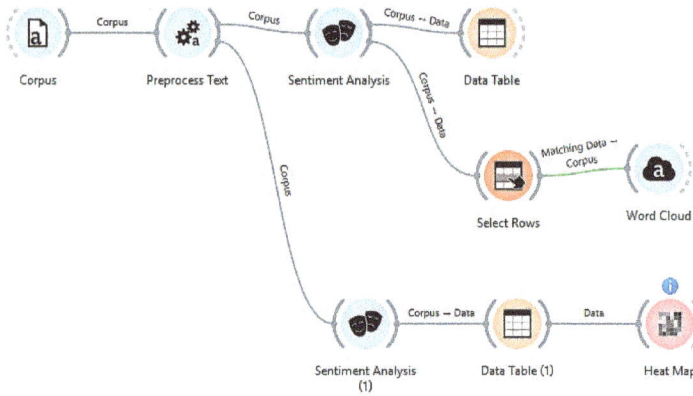

Open the heat map, choose a color gradient, cluster by rows and annotate it with the text.

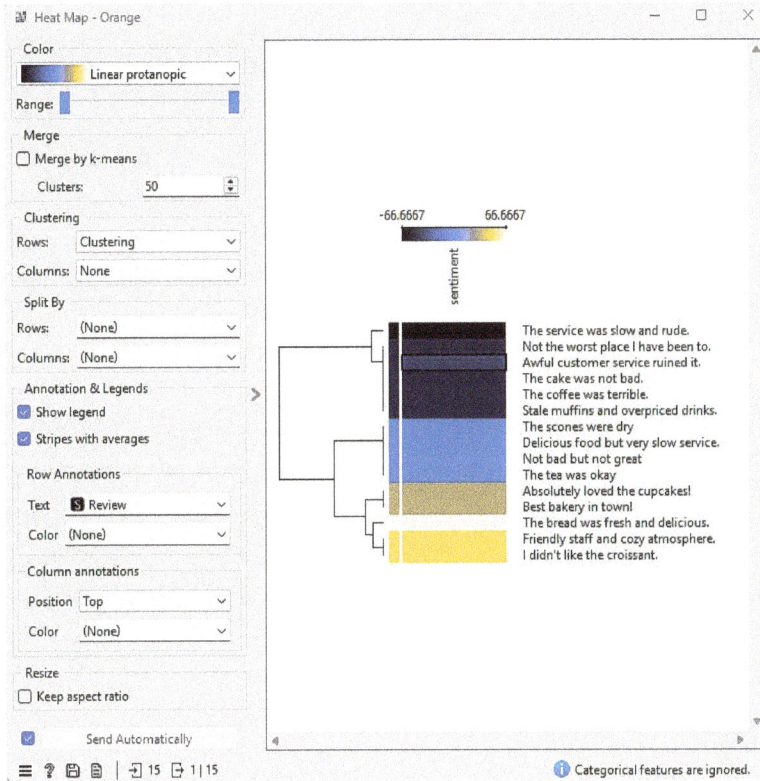

The heat map visual gives a view of the sentiment results coded by a color gradient and grouped and ordered by sentiment scores.

5.2 Wrap-Up

To summarize, in this lab you learned how to perform rule-based sentiment analysis using two methods: VADER and Liu-Hu (LH).

These both use lexicon rules to determine the emotional tone of a text. They differ in how they handle language and score. VADER considers contextual cues like punctuation, capitalization, and negation, making it more effective for short and informal texts. LH is simpler, relying strictly on word counts from positive and negative lists.

You applied these methods to real text data, examined numerical sentiment scores, and visualized results. While rule-based methods are useful for straightforward tasks, more complex language understanding often requires machine learning techniques, which will be explored in the next lab.

5.3 Exercises

Sentiment Analysis (Rule-Based)

In this exercise, you will apply rule-based sentiment analysis. You will explore and compare sentiment scores across different datasets and visualize results using tables, heatmaps, and word clouds.

Dataset 1: tech_support_tweets.csv

This dataset includes short social media posts (tweets) about technology products or services. Each row contains a short text snippet from a customer.

1. What is the overall sentiment of the tweet: "Your app update broke everything. Thanks."? (Answer with sentiment label and compound score)

2. Find one tweet with a positive compound score. Paste the tweet and its score.

3. Use the Word Cloud to show the most common words in negative tweets. Paste a screenshot of your word cloud.

4. Find a tweet with both high positive and high negative scores. What is the sentiment label assigned? Do you agree? Why or why not?

5. Now use the LH method on the same dataset. Compare the LH and VADER sentiment scores for one mixed-emotion tweet. Do they agree?

Dataset 2: student_feedback.csv

This dataset contains open-ended feedback from students about a university course.

6. What is the LH sentiment score for the comment: "Loved the instructor, but the class moved too fast"?

7. In the Heat Map, which feedback comment appears most negative? Paste the comment.

8. Cluster the Heat Map by rows. Do comments with similar sentiment scores group together?

9. Use Select Rows to filter for positive comments. Paste a Word Cloud of common positive words.

10. Based on LH results, what is the average sentiment score across all feed-back comments? (Use "Distributions" widget or calculate manually)

Dataset 3: product_complaints.csv

This dataset includes product complaints submitted to a company.

11. Which complaint has the strongest negative LH sentiment score? Paste the complaint and score.

12. Create a Word Cloud of positive complaint terms (if any). Paste a screen-shot.

13. Compare LH and VADER for the complaint: "Amazing design, terrible durability." Do they agree?

14. In the Heat Map, do complaints about the same product cluster together? Paste a screenshot and explain.

15. Write one sentence summarizing how LH and VADER differ when ana-lyzing emotional tone in customer complaints.

Lab 6

Sentiment Analysis (Machine Learning Based)

When you're trying to figure out whether a sentence or paragraph sounds positive, negative, or somewhere in the middle, that's where sentiment analysis comes in. There are a couple of different ways to do this. One of the older, simpler ones is rule-based — you rely on word lists and a bunch of preset rules.

But there's another approach - using machine learning. Instead of depending on fixed rules, this involves training the computer from real examples. For example supplying it with lots of reviews that have already been labeled with how people felt. The model looks for patterns in those examples and uses them to make guesses about new text. This makes it a lot better at handling messy language, casual wording, and stuff you might see online or in real reviews.

So, what is machine learning exactly? It's part of artificial intelligence, and it's all about letting computers learn from data. You don't tell the system exactly what to do — instead, it picks up patterns and uses those to make decisions. There are two big types: supervised learning, where the system learns from examples with answers already provided, and unsupervised learning, where it tries to group or organize things without knowing the correct labels ahead of time.

For this lab, you'll be using the supervised kind — specifically, to train a sentiment analysis model.

You'll do all of this in Orange, which is a visual tool for working with data (no coding needed). The dataset includes short text reviews that are already marked as positive, negative, or neutral. You'll guide the model by showing it these labeled examples.

6.1   Lesson Steps

Step 1: Load the Dataset

Open a new Orange workflow and put a File widget on the canvas. Add the file 'generic_reviews.csv' and set as shown. VERY important make sure the sentiment column is set to 'target' (this can be changed by pulling down the row option).

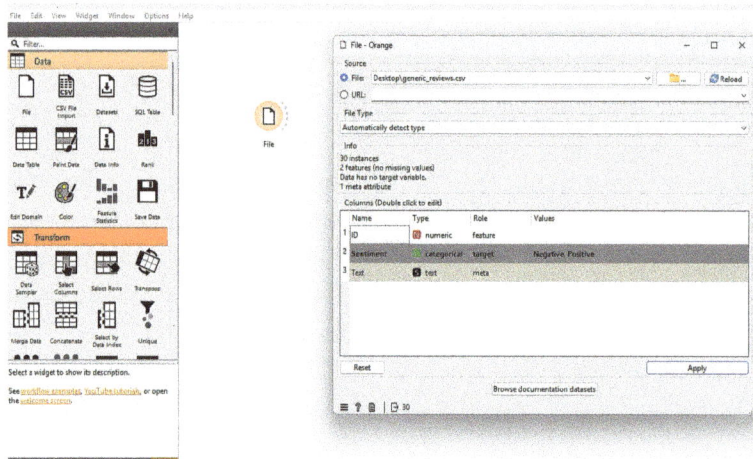

Step 2: Create a Corpus

A Corpus data object is needed for the data to be in the correct format for Orange to perform NLP analysis. Add a Corpus widget to the workflow and connect it to the File widget.

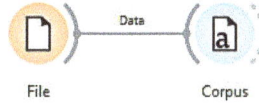

Step 3: Preprocess

Add and connect the Preprocess Text widget to the corpus widget and set it as depicted. This will convert the data to lowercase, tokenize it and remove stopwords.

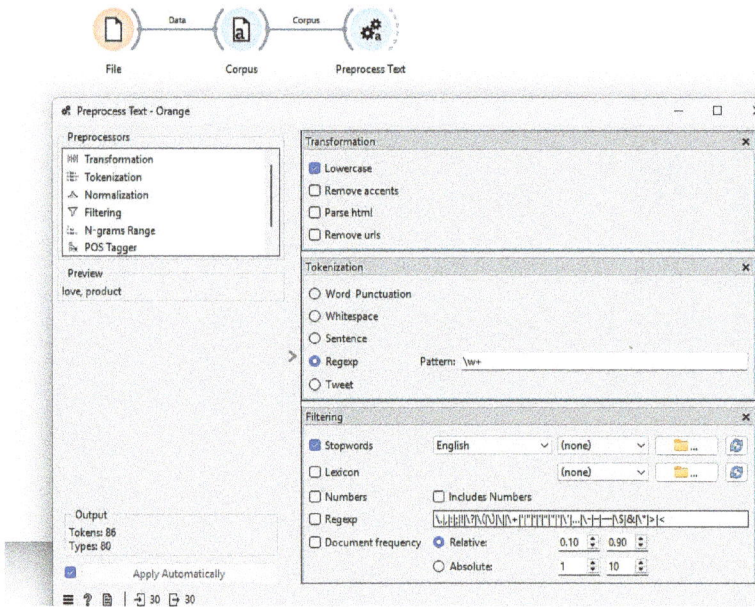

Step 4: Encode

Add a Bag of Words widget to the workflow and connect it to the Preprocess Text widget. Open this and set it to IDF for the document frequency (it default to bag of words method which you do not want to use here).

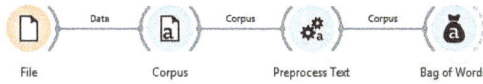

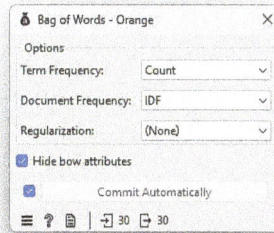

Step 5: Sampling

Because we want to be able to evaluate our classification (machine learning algorithm) we need to split out data into test (to evaluate) and train (to make the model) subsets of data randomly selected. To do this add a Data Sampler widget and set the proportion of data sampled to 70%.

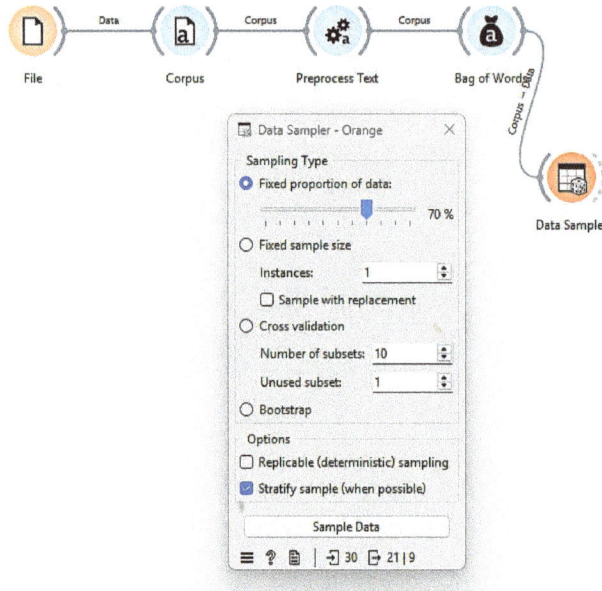

Step 6: Set up Classification

To set up the classifier we will run the 70% of the data through the logistic regression model (our classification algorithm we will use here) and 30% to test. To do this add a Logistic Regression widget to the workflow and flow the data sample (training data) to this (see connector details below).

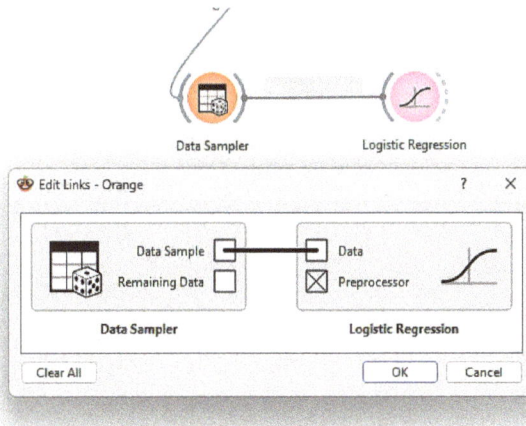

Next add a Test and Score widget, connect this to the Logistic Regression widget. Also connect the Data Sampler widget to the Test and Score widget and set the connector for this to send test data - aka Remaining Data (the 30% reserved test data not the 70% training data going to the logistic model) to the Test and Score widget. Make sure the connectors are set properly with the correct data being passed.

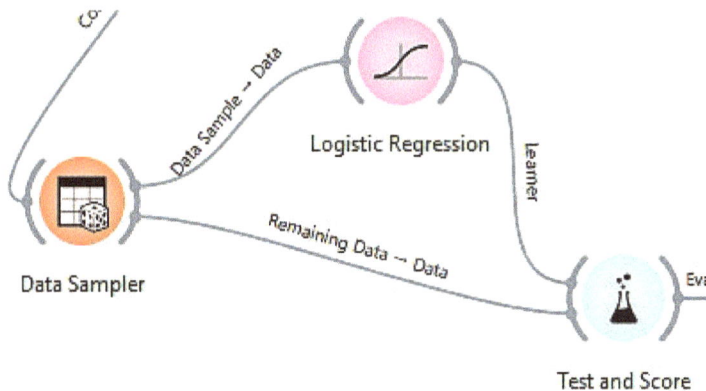

In this setup, the training data (data sample) goes through the logistic regression model to make the model based on the training data. The model is sent to the test and score (parameters are used for evaluating the test data). The test data (remaing data) is sent to the test and score (but does not go through the logistic model as it is not involved in making the model) and used to evaluate the model.

Step 7: View Results

View results by clicking on the Test and Score widget. (NOTE this is based sampling and results will vary, go back to the sampler widget and resample to see how this works).

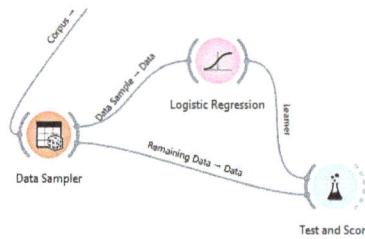

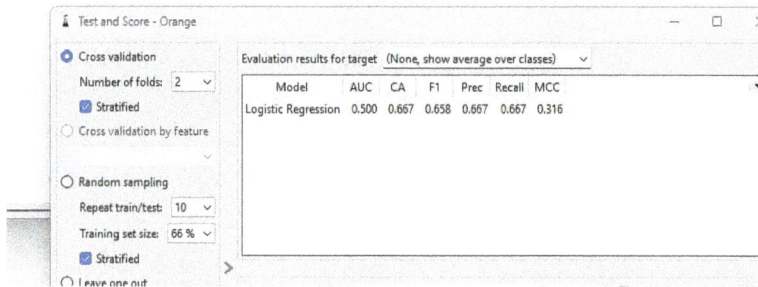

This result shows how well a logistic regression model performed on your dataset using cross-validation. The model correctly predicted the outcome about 67% of the time, which seems decent at first. However, the AUC score is 0.5, meaning the model isn't actually good at distinguishing between positive and negative cases—it's basically guessing. While the precision, recall, and F1 score are consistent at around 66%, the low AUC suggests the model might not be very useful, possibly due to imbalanced data or not enough meaningful features.

Also add a Confusion Matrix to the Test and Score matrix to review results in this form (easier and more familiar to understand).

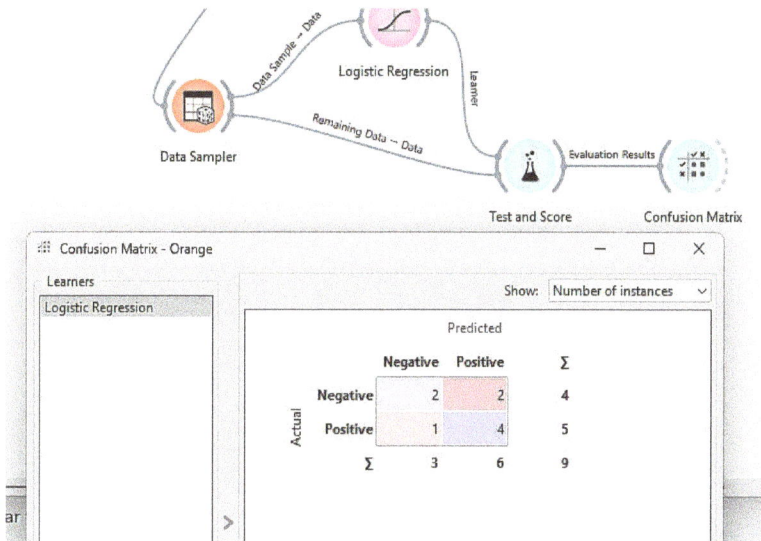

The confusion matrix shows that the logistic regression model made 9 predictions in total. Out of these, it correctly predicted 2 negative and 4 positive cases, resulting in 6 accurate predictions. However, it also made 3 mistakes— 2 negative cases were incorrectly predicted as positive (false positives), and 1 positive case was predicted as negative (false negative). Overall, the model achieved an accuracy of about 67%, which aligns with the earlier evaluation. While the model shows some ability to distinguish between the two classes, the small sample size means the results may not be very reliable or generalizable.

6.2 Wrap-Up

In this lab, you built a sentiment analysis model based on methods of machine learning. You practiced loading the data, cleaning it up, turning the text into numbers with TF-IDF, and then training a logistic regression model. Finally, you checked how well it worked using accuracy, AUC, and the confusion matrix.

The idea was to show how a machine learning model can learn to spot patterns in the data — like which kinds of words usually go with positive or negative reviews — and then use that to make predictions. Unlike rule-based methods, this one isn't just following a fixed list of words, so it's more flexible.

6.3   Exercises

Sentiment Analysis (Machine Learning Based)

This exercise will practice machine learning based sentiment analysis.

Dataset 1: Amazon Pet Product Reviews

This dataset pet_product_reviews.csv includes short reviews of pet products (e.g., dog food, cat toys) from Amazon, each labeled as "positive" or "negative".

1. Paste a screenshot or describe the TF-IDF settings used in your Bag of Words widget.
2. What percentage of reviews were correctly predicted by your logistic regression model? (Paste the accuracy score from the Test & Score widget.)
3. Paste the AUC value from your model evaluation.
4. Interpret your confusion matrix: How many false positives and false negatives were there?
5. Re-run the Data Sampler (resample) and record how your accuracy and AUC scores changed. Why might they differ?

Dataset 2: YouTube Video Comments

This dataset youtube_comments.csv contains comments on various YouTube videos, labeled with sentiment ("positive", "negative", or "neutral").

Make sure to set the "sentiment" column as the target. You may choose to filter out "neutral" labels to simplify binary classification.

6. What preprocessing steps did you apply to the text data? List the selected options from the Preprocess Text widget.
7. After converting to TF-IDF, how many features (tokens/words) were generated? (View in Bag of Words output.)
8. What was your logistic regression model's accuracy on this dataset?
9. Paste or summarize your confusion matrix results for this dataset.
10. What could be contributing to misclassifications in this dataset (e.g., informal language, sarcasm)?

Lab 7

Topic Modeling - Latent Dirichlet Allocation

Topic modeling is a way to figure out the general subjects are in a bunch of documents — without needing someone to tag or label anything first. It's part of natural language processing, and the method looks for patterns in how words show up together.

Unlike clustering (which this method is related to but clustering is for numeric data), which puts a document in one group only, topic modeling is a bit more flexible. A single piece of text can be connected to more than one topic, which makes sense since real writing often touches on more than one idea.

LDA — short for latent Dirichlet allocation - is a topic modelling method that is a kind of statistical model that assumes each document is a mix of several topics, and each topic is made up of a mix of words. The algorithm doesn't know what any of it means at first — it just looks at which words tend to show up together. For example, if it sees "planet," "NASA," and "rocket" in a lot of the same places, it might decide there's a topic about space, even if the word "space" never appears.

In this lab, you'll try out LDA using Orange. You'll start with a small set of sample texts, clean them up a bit, turn the words into numbers using Bag of Words, and then apply the LDA model. After that, you can take a closer look at the topics it finds and see what makes sense. There are a few ways to check how good the topics are — stuff like coherence and perplexity. Even though you'll be working with a small dataset here, it should give you a pretty good feel for how the method works and why it's useful when you've got a lot of text to sort through.

7.1   Lesson Steps

Step 1: Loading the Data

Open a new workflow in Orange. Add a Corpus widget from the Text Mining section to the canvas (if this is your first lab you may need to install this section as an add in).

Open the Corpus widget and upload the topics.csv file containing your documents. Make sure to select the correct column that contains the text data as the content to be analyzed.

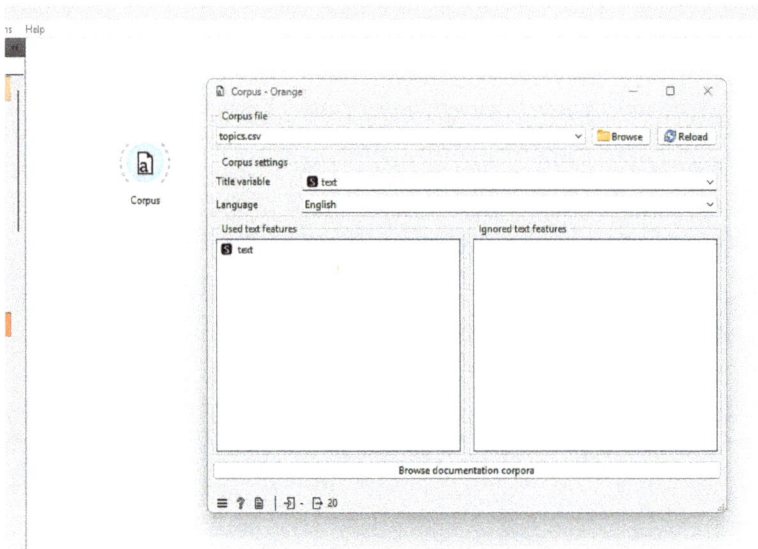

Step 2: Preprocess the Text

Add a Preprocess Text (note this is NOT the Preprocess widget from the transform menu but the one in the Text Mining menu) widget to your workflow. Connect this to the Corpus widget.

In the settings in the Preprocess Text widget, set Transformation to lowercase. For Tokenization, choose word. Keep Filtering at the default setting to remove stop words. Then, add normalization and select WordNet Lemmatizer.

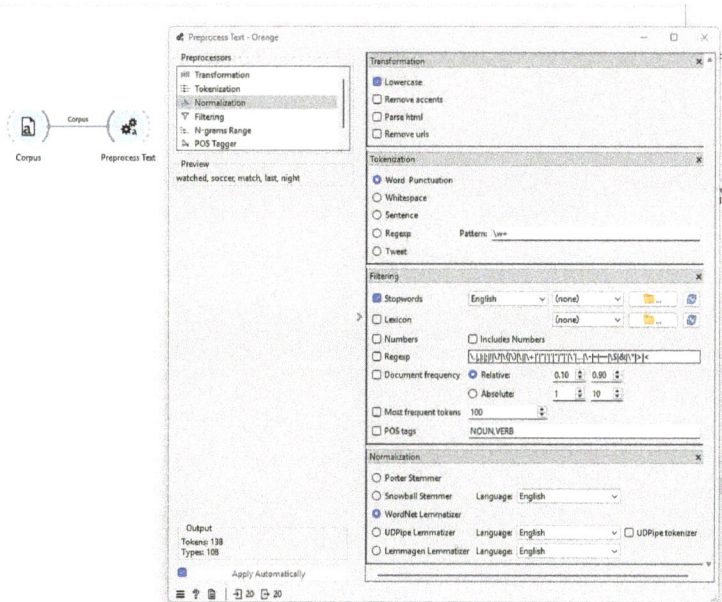

Step 3: Encode the Data

Add a Bag of Words widget to the workflow. Connect it to the Preprocess Text widget. Open the settings and set Document Frequency to IDF instead of raw count.

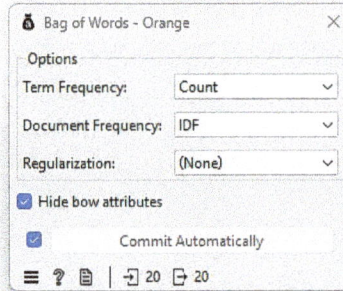

Step 4: Apply LDA Topic Modeling

Add a Topic Modeling widget to the workflow. Connect it to the Bag of Words. In the settings, choose the method Latent Dirichlet Allocation. Set the number of topics to start with 4.

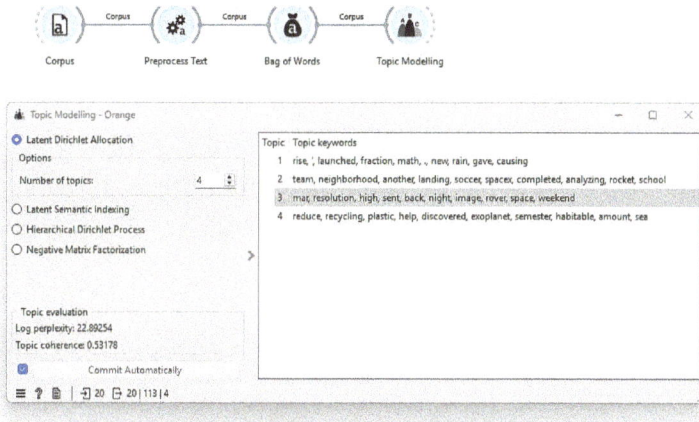

You can observe the results in the output panel of the Topic Modeling widget. Presented there are the top words associated with each topic, along with evaluation metrics like topic coherence and log perplexity. The evaluation metric topic coherence indicates how meaningful the topics are by measuring relative distance between words. The log perplexity metric measures how well the model predicts the data. For coherence higher is better and for log perplexity lower is better.

Topic 1 appears to have a mix of topics from education and the environment, with words like math, fraction, rise, and rain pointing to school subjects and climate-related concepts. Topic 2 mixes elements of sports and space, combining terms such as team, soccer, and neighborhood with spacex, rocket, and landing. Topic 3 is apprently on space exploration, with strong keywords like mars, rover, image, resolution, and space. Topic 4 reflects environmental topics, including recycling, plastic, and sea, but also includes some crossover from space (exoplanet, habitable) and education (semester).

Step 5: Interpret the Results

Making sense LDA results can be confusing, especially if the text it is using as input is diverse. It is an unsupervised technique doesn't use any labels ahead of time, so it is largely exploratory. LDA just looks at how words show up together — and that can lead to topics that feel mixed or not clear.

Even when you think the documents are clearly grouped, the model can still mash things together. Like, "school" and "team" might both show up in stuff about sports and education, so they get pulled into the same topic. With just 20 documents, there's really not enough material for the model to sort things cleanly anyway. Plus, if a sentence talks about more than one thing — like sports and school in the same breath — that just confuses things more. You end up with topics that don't feel all that separate.

Step 6: Save Workflow

If you are doing lab 8 it is a continuation of lab 7 so safe this workflow as a *.ows file in a handy location you can reopen it from later.

7.2 Wrap-Up

In this lab, we examined how Latent Dirichlet Allocation (LDA) can be used to identify underlying themes in a corpus of documents. LDA is a commonly used method for exploring topics without prior labels, making sense of the output can be tricky. Since the algorithm is based on how words appear together rather than on any fixed categories, the topics it generates can sometimes be unclear or overlap — especially when dealing with limited or varied data. Nevertheless, it remains a helpful way to get a better sense of the structure and major ideas present in your text.

7.3 Exercises

Topic Modeling - Latent Dirichlet Allocation

The purpose of this exercise is to get hands-on practice using LDA to uncover topics in real-world text data.

Dataset 1: Movie Reviews (movie_reviews.csv)

This data is a sampling of movie reviews from different genres, such as romance, action, and science fiction.

1. Load and preprocess the data and run the LDA. What are the most prominent words that show up under Topic 1 in the LDA results?

2. How many topics did you ask the model to find? Try adjusting the number and note what changes. How does this affect how clearly the topics make sense?

3. What does the topic coherence score tell you about how well your topics are formed?

4. Take a look at the top words in Topic 2. Can you guess which genre this topic is related to?

5. When reviewing the topic mix for individual documents, do any of the reviews seem to connect to multiple topics?

Dataset 2: News Headlines (news_headlines.csv)

This dataset includes short news headlines from categories like sports, tech, and politics.

6. Load the data and preprocess the data and run LDA. How do the main words in Topic 3 here compare to Topic 1?

7. Which topic seems to center around sports content? Share at least three keywords that point you in that direction.

8. When comparing results, what makes it challenging to interpret topics from short texts (like headlines) compared to full-length reviews?

9. What happens to the log perplexity value when you raise the number of topics from 3 to 5?

10. Based on your findings, how does LDA manage documents that touch on more than one subject or theme?

Lab 8

Comparing Topic Modeling Methods

In Lab 7, you worked directly with Latent Dirichlet Allocation (LDA), one of the more common tools for finding topics in text. In this lab, we try out two other approaches that are also used for topic modeling.

Non-negative Matrix Factorization (NMF) uses methodology from linear algebra and will often produces topics that are easier to interpret at a glance. Latent Semantic Analysis (LSA) also uses linear algebra but to reduce dimensionality in the data and capture underlying structure from there. Sometimes LSA can be useful for identifying broader latent concepts (such as 'news').

In this lab, you will apply all three methods using the same dataset and compare results on how the perform topic modelling.

8.1 Lesson Steps

Step 1: Open Workflow

Open this workflow you saved from 7.

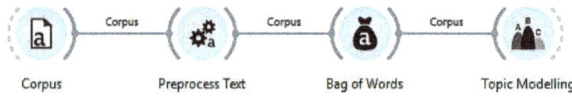

Step 2: Topic Modeling- NM

Add another Topic Modeling widget to your workflow. Connect it to the Bag of Words widget, just like you did before. Inside this new Topic Modelling widget, choose the method called Non-negative Matrix Factorization. Set the number of topics to 4, the same as in the previous step.

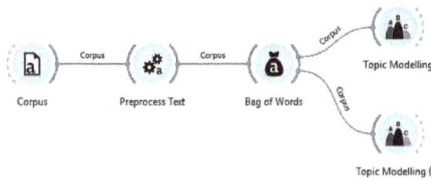

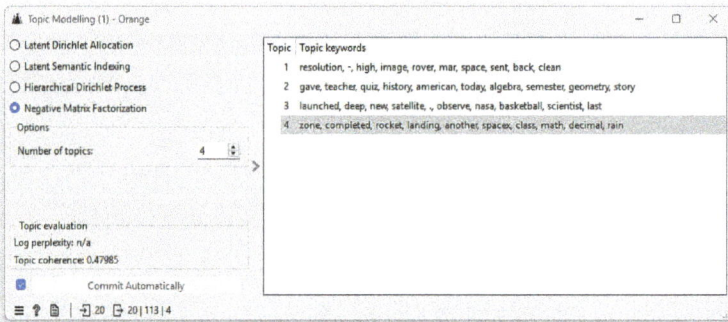

After the model runs, look at the list of words for each topic. Compare these

words to the topics you got from the LDA method. Also, check the topic coherence score to see how well the topics make sense.

Step 3: Topic Modeling Widget - LSA

Add a third Topic Modeling widget to your workflow. Connect it to the Bag
of Words widget. In the widget settings, select the method Latent Semantic
Indexing (LSA) and set the number of topics to 4.

Once the model finishes running, open it up and look at the top words for each topic. Also, check the topic coherence score to see how well the topics make sense.

Step 4: Compare the Results

Go ahead and open each Topic Modeling widget in Orange. Look at the words it shows for each topic — the main ones near the top. This will give you a quick sense of what each topic is probably about.

Now check the topic coherence score. It should be there in the widget too. That number tells you if the words in a topic sort of belong together. If it's higher, that usually means the topic makes more sense overall.

After that, think about which method makes the differences between topics the most clear. Look at both the key words and the coherence scores when deciding. The strongest method will usually show distinct themes that are easy to recognize.

8.2   Wrap-Up

In this lab, you worked with three different topic modeling techniques—LDA, NMF, and LSA—on the same dataset to see how each one uncovers patterns in text. Although they're all designed to find underlying themes in text, they approach the task in different ways. Consequently, differences show up in the kinds of results they produce.

Looking at the top keywords and comparing how coherent the topics were, you got a sense of how to evaluate what each model is telling you. There's no one-size-fits-all solution here—the right method depends on what you're trying to achieve. Whether you're after clarity, speed, or deeper patterns, knowing the trade-offs of each approach gives you a better foundation for making smart choices in future projects.

8.3 Exercises

Comparing Topic Modeling Methods

Let's practice and compare methods of topic modeling. You will apply all three methods on the same datasets, compare their topic outputs, and evaluate topic coherence and interpretability.

Note this lab uses the same data as prior lab.

Dataset 1: Movie Reviews

1. Begin by loading the movie_reviews.csv file. Clean up the text — make everything lowercase, break it into tokens, remove stopwords, and lemmatize the words. After that, turn the text into a Bag of Words representation.

2. Use LDA to extract 4 topics. Look at the top five words from each topic. Based on those keywords, which topics might be connected to romance, action, or sci-fi films? Briefly explain how you matched them.

3. Run NMF on the same data using 4 topics again. Compare the top words for each topic with the ones from LDA. In your view, which model gave you more clearly defined or understandable topics?

4. Now try LSA with 4 topics. Check out the top terms for each group. Are these groupings more specific, broader, or just different from the ones created by LDA and NMF? Which ones made the most sense to you?

5. Take a look at the topic coherence scores for all three models. Which one scored the highest on this dataset?

6. Thinking about what you've seen so far, which of the three methods would you pick for analyzing movie reviews?

Dataset 2: News Headlines

7. Go ahead and clean up the text in news_headlines.csv the same way you did before—lowercase it, get rid of stopwords, tokenize, lemmatize, all that. Once that's done, build your Bag of Words version.

8. Run LDA with 4 topics. Take a look at the top 5 words that come out for each one. Do any of them feel like they're about politics? Maybe one leans toward sports or tech? Jot down your guesses and explain what

made you think that.

9. Now switch over to NMF—again, stick with 4 topics. Check out the top words from this one too. Are they similar to what LDA gave you, or is it picking up on something different?

10. Time to try LSA with the same setup. Look at the keywords in each topic. Compared to the others, do these feel a little broader? Or are they zooming in more on specific ideas? Just give your honest take.

11. Look at the coherence scores from all three models. Which one came out on top for this set? Write it down—it might surprise you.

12. Since headlines are usually pretty short and straight to the point, which of these three methods do you think handles them best? Use what you saw in the topics and coherence to back up your pick.

Lab 9

Text Classification (Naive Bayes)

Classifying text means organizing written content into specific categories based on what it says. This process plays a big role in natural language processing and shows up in things like filtering spam emails, figuring out if a review is positive or negative, and labeling topics in articles. Classification always works on encoded data - text turned into numbers. This is how a machine learning algorithm can pick up on patterns that help tell different categories apart.

In this lab, we're going to work with a classification method called Naive Bayes. It's a relatively simple approach using Bayes theorem (yes the same one from intro statistics) that's surprisingly effective for sorting text. Naive Bayes is based on Bayes' theorem and makes the assumption that each word in a document contributes to the final decision independently. Even though that assumption doesn't always hold up in real-world language, the algorithm still tends to perform quite well in many cases.

You'll be using Orange to build and test your Naive Bayes classifier. The process includes loading in some text data, preparing it, converting the words into a Bag of Words format, and training the model. Once that's done, you'll test how well it can predict the category of new text. It's a hands-on way to get a feel for how text classification works using a simple but powerful tool.

9.1 Lesson Steps

Step 1: Load Data

Start by launching Orange and creating a new project. Drag the File widget onto your workspace and open the file named spam.csv. Within the widget settings, assign the message column as the text field—this tells Orange that this is the content to analyze. Then mark the label column as a categorical feature, since it represents the category (spam or not) that we're aiming to predict.

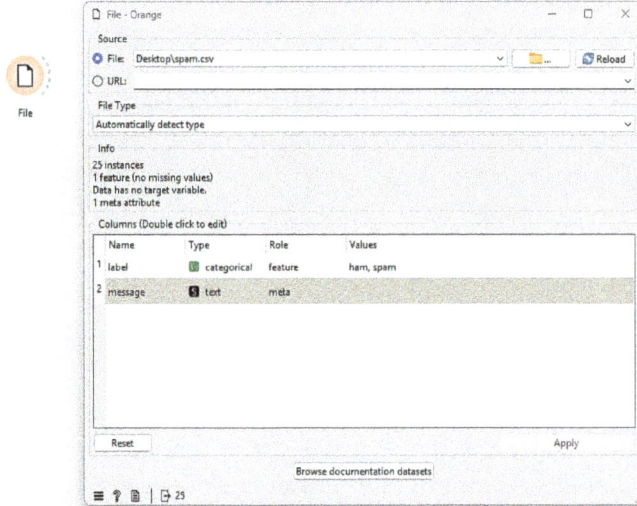

Step 2: Select the Target variable

Add a select columns widget and choose the target variable 'label'.

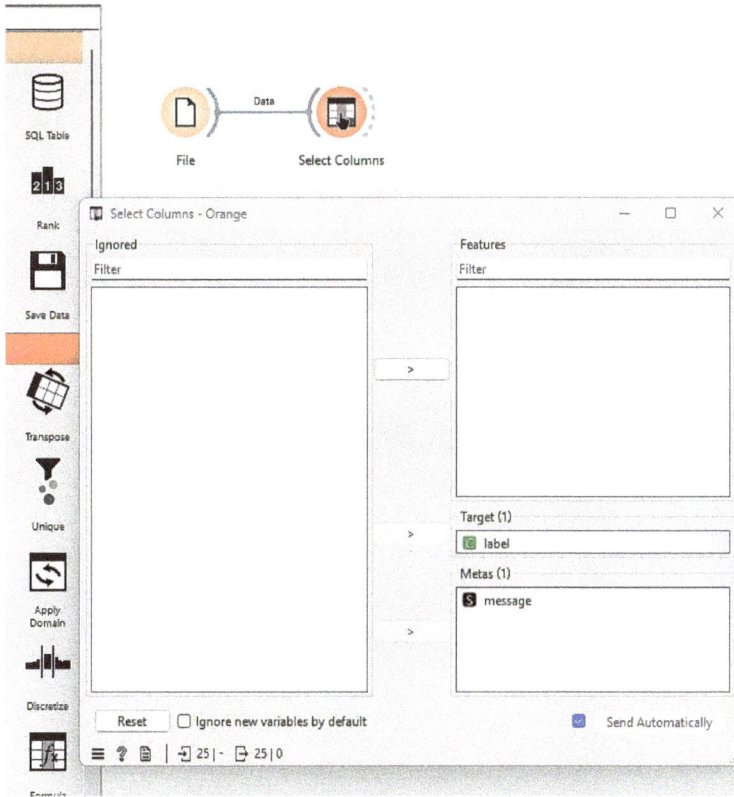

Step 3: Create a Corpus

To prepare the data for text processing, insert a Corpus widget and connect it to the column selector. Inside the Corpus widget, specify message as the text source. For a closer look at the data, you can also add a Corpus Viewer and link it to the Corpus widget to scroll through individual entries.

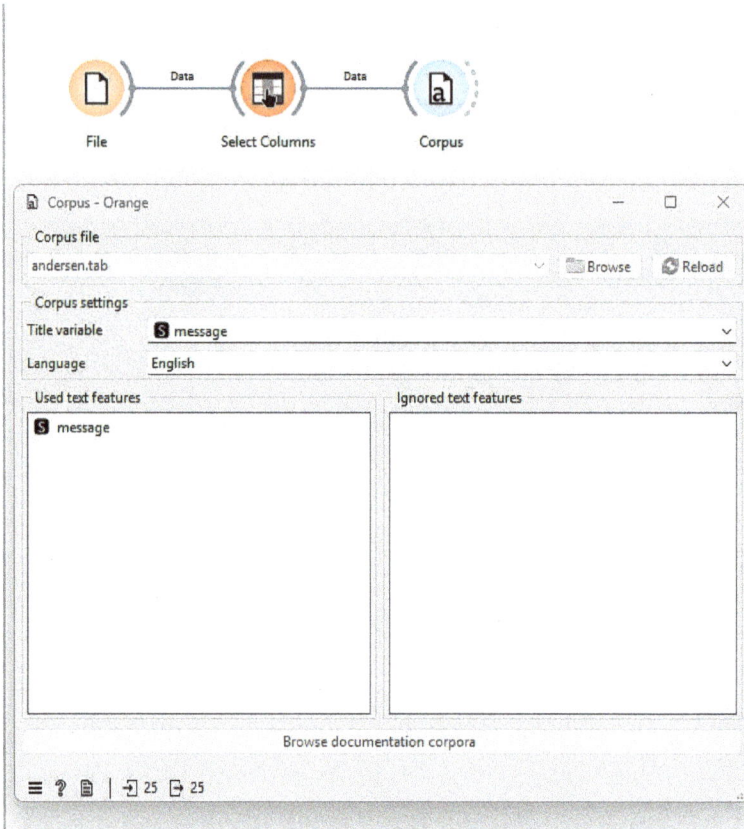

Step 4: Preprocess the Text

Add a Preprocess Text widget to the workflow. Next connect it to the Corpus widget. In the Preprocess Text settings, enable lowercase conversion and tokenize using the regular expression. Then, remove English stopwords. Apply a filter to keep only words that appear in 10 to 90 percent of the documents. Limit the vocabulary to the top 100 most frequent words. Finally, use part-of-speech tagging to retain only nouns and verbs. See the figure below.

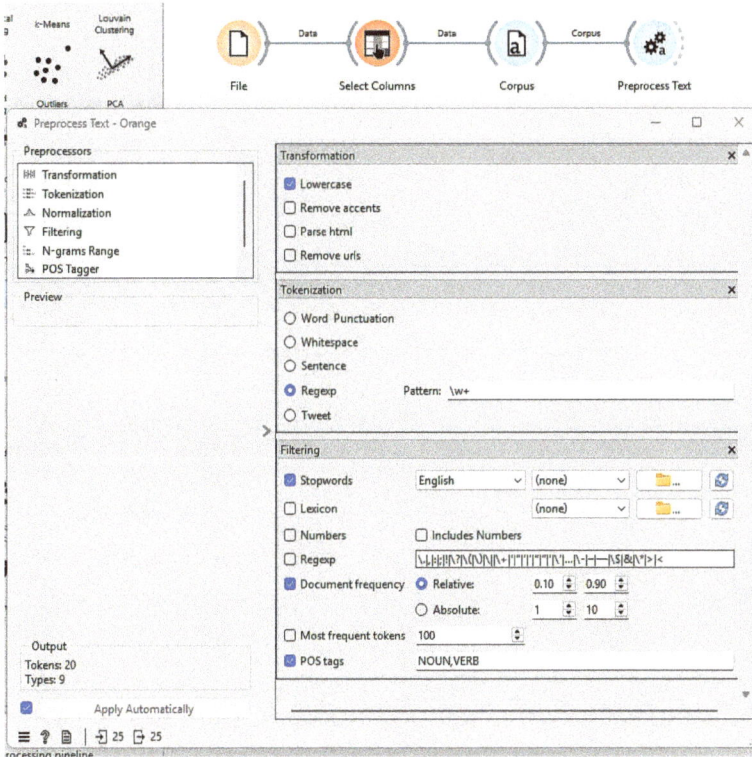

Step 5: Encode Text Using Bag of Words

Now, drop a Bag of Words widget into the workspace and link it to the Preprocess Text widget. Inside the configuration, activate the TF-IDF weighting option. This step ensures that common terms across all messages get less weight, while rarer but informative words become more important.

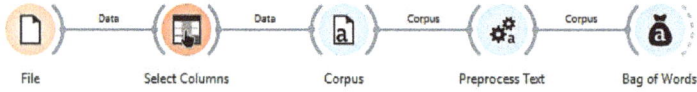

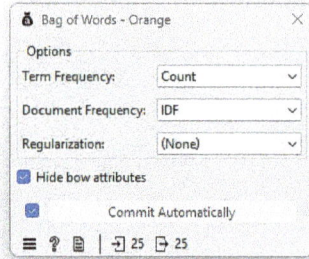

To see how the text data has been converted into numerical form, add a Data Table widget and connect it to the Bag of Words output. This view lets you explore the resulting word features for each message.

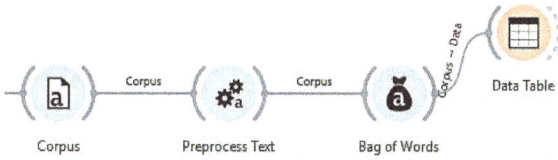

Step 6: Split the Data

To prepare for training and testing, use the Data Sampler widget. Attach it to the Bag of Words output. Set the sampling ratio so that 70% of the data is used for training. The other 30% will be held back for evaluating how well the model performs.

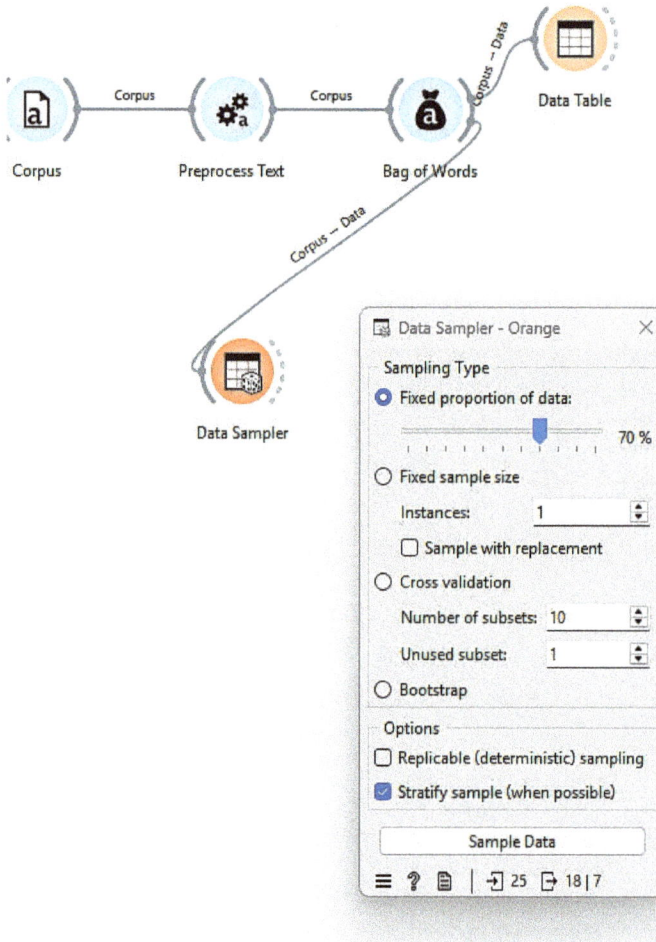

Step 7: Train and Evaluate with Naive Baye

Next, drag the Naive Bayes widget into your flow and connect it to the output labeled "Data Sample" from the Data Sampler. This section of the data will be used to train the model.

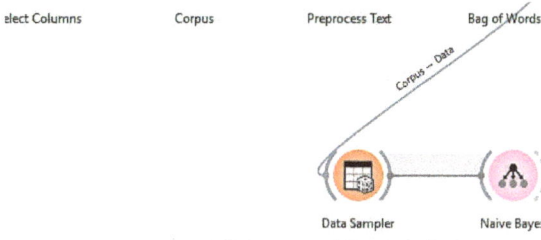

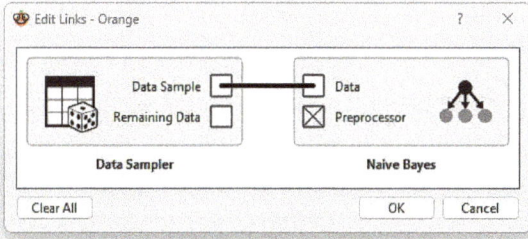

Now bring in the Test and Score widget. Link the Naive Bayes model to it, and also connect the "Remaining Data" output from the Data Sampler. This connection ensures that the test data goes directly to the evaluation stage, without affecting the training process.

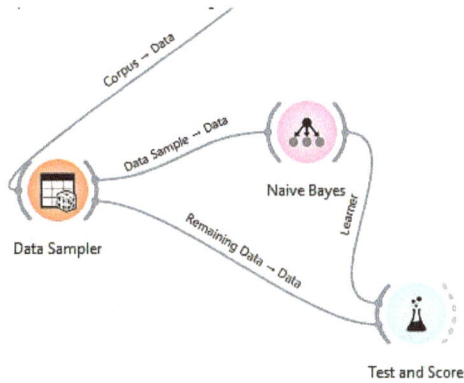

In this setup, 70 percent of the messages are used to build the model using Naive Bayes. The trained model is then passed to the Test and Score widget. At the same time, the remaining 30 percent of data is sent directly to the same widget for evaluation. Because it bypasses the Naive Bayes block, the test set stays untouched by the training step and is used strictly to measure performance.

Step 8: Analyze Results

Open the Test and Score widget to check key performance metrics. You'll find values such as accuracy, precision, recall, F1 score, and AUC. Among these, the Classification Accuracy (CA) score is especially useful—it reflects how many messages were classified correctly. In this run, accuracy came out to 57%, though this number can change based on how the data was split.

To dive deeper into how the model performed, attach a Confusion Matrix widget. Open it to see where the predictions went wrong—for example, which spam messages were misclassified as non-spam or vice versa. In this example, 3 out of the 7 test messages were incorrectly labeled. Results will differ each time due to the randomness of the data split.

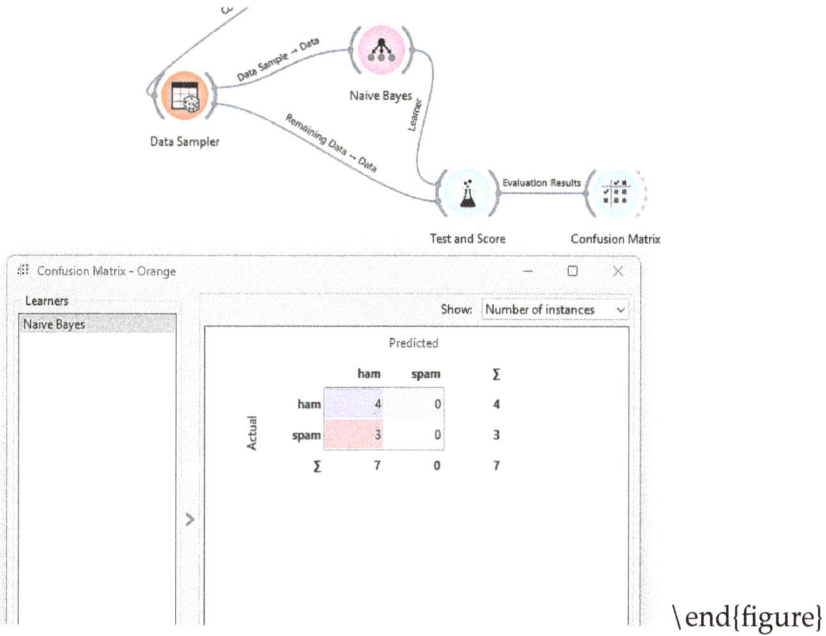

\end{figure}

9.2 Wrap-Up

This lab walked through the steps of creating a simple text classification pipeline using Orange. Starting from loading and cleaning the raw text, you moved through transforming that data using TF-IDF with Bag of Words, and then trained a Naive Bayes model to make predictions. The performance wasn't particularly high, which is expected with a small dataset and randomized split. Still, it's a solid introduction to how basic machine learning workflows can be applied to real-world text data.

This exercise gives you a foundation in handling textual data for classification tasks—an essential part of natural language processing.

9.3   Exercises

Naive Bayes Text Classification

Let's practice text classification using Naive Bayes.

Dataset 1: Customer Support Tickets

Use the file support_tickets.csv.

1. Paste the classification accuracy and AUC score from Test & Score.
2. Which label had more misclassifications? How many?
3. Adjust preprocessing to keep only nouns. Did performance improve or drop?
4. Lower top vocabulary size from 100 to 50. What changed in accuracy?
5. In your own words, why might some tickets be hard to classify?

Dataset 2: Movie Review Sentiment

Use the file movie_sentiment.csv.

6. What is the classifier's accuracy and F1 score?
7. Which sentiment (positive or negative) is easier for the model to predict?
8. Change preprocessing to include only adjectives. What changes in model accuracy?
9. Looking at misclassified examples, why might they be hard to judge?
10. Use the Corpus Viewer to list 3 common words in positive reviews.